Yoga

A BEGINNER'S GUIDE

GEORG & BRENDA FEUERSTEIN

JAICO PUBLISHING HOUSE

Ahmedabad Bangalore Chennai
Delhi Hyderabad Kolkata Mumbai

Published by Jaico Publishing House
A-2 Jash Chambers, 7-A Sir Phirozshah Mehta Road
Fort, Mumbai - 400 001
jaicopub@jaicobooks.com
www.jaicobooks.com

Published in arrangement with
Hohm Press
P.O. Box 4410, Chino Valley
AZ 86323, USA

Authorized edition for sale in India, Bangladesh,
Bhutan, Pakistan, Nepal, Sri Lanka and the Maldives.

YOGA: A BEGINNER'S GUIDE
ISBN 978-81-8495-624-5

First Jaico Impression: 2014

Printed by
Trinity Academy For Corporate Training Limited, Mumbai

CONTENTS

Foreword by Judith Hanson Lasater....ix

Preface....xiii

PART ONE: Exploring the Tradition of Yoga....1

1. Introducing Yoga....3
2. The Secret of Change....6
3. The Mind: Agent of Change....8
4. Traditional Yoga Today....10
5. The Twelve Steps of Spiritual Recovery....12
6. Suffering Beyond Pain....15
7. Raja-Yoga: The Path of Contemplation....18
8. Hatha-Yoga: The Path of Physical Transformation....24
9. Jnana-Yoga: The Path of Knowledge....27
10. Karma-Yoga: The Path of Ego-Free Action....30
11. Bhakti-Yoga: The Path of the Heart....32
12. Mantra-Yoga: The Path of Potent Sound....34

13. Tantra-Yoga: The Path of Continuity....36

14. The Teacher: Helper on the Threshold....38

15. The Disciple: Pilgrim to Reality....41

16. The Path: The Way to Spiritual Freedom....43

17. Predictable Obstacles....45

18. Self-Discipline: Necessary Restraint....48

19. Community: Strength in Numbers....51

20. Ego-Transcendence: Beyond I, Me, and Mine....53

21. Wisdom....56

22. Proper Livelihood: Integrity in All Matters....59

23. Diet: You are What You Eat....61

24. Liberation: Spiritual Freedom....63

PART TWO: Questions and Answers....65

Prelude....67

1. I am a Christian....67

2. I am strongly drawn to Hinduism....68

3. Where can I find a guru?....69

4. Why do you write Yoga with a capital Y?....69

5. My partner has no interest in Yoga....70

6. I have a very busy life....70

7. I like meat....70

8. When I read Yoga texts....71
9. Sometimes I just don't have the time, which makes me feel very guilty....71
10. My mind is racing....72
11. I think that Yoga is self-hypnosis....72
12. My problem is: I easily fall of the wagon....73
13. There are many things I don't like about my guru....73
14. I am an atheist....75
15. Do I really need a guru?....75
16. I find living liberation difficult to understand....76
17. Some forms of Yoga seem to accept a belief in God....77
18. If the *yogis* are so realistic....78
19. Is it okay to charge for Yoga instruction?....78
20. I was shocked to see women dressed in rather skimpy and provocative outfits....79
21. The Yoga studio that I normally go to is forever marketing Yoga products....80
22. I find it disturbing that so many studios play music during class....80
23. I used to enjoy Partner Yoga....81
24. Where can I find spiritually based Yoga classes?....81
25. Where in India should I go to learn Yoga properly?....82

26. Have you any additional comments about Yoga's role in creating a healthier environment? 83

27. I heard in a seminar that the ego must be killed before enlightenment can happen. Is this true? 84

28. Why is it that we hear a lot about male Yoga teachers 84

29. How can I make posture practice a *spiritual* affair? 85

30. I have a Buddhist meditation practice and also do Hatha-Yoga postures occasionally 85

APPENDIXES 87

Appendix A: A Guide to Sanskrit Pronunciation 89

Appendix B: What to Read and Study Next? 90

SELECT BIBLIOGRAPHY 95

ESSENTIAL SANSKRIT GLOSSARY 99

INDEX 109

ABOUT THE AUTHORS 127

FOREWORD

We are often warned to be careful about what we wish for because we just might get it, and with that "success" come inevitable, unpredictable, and unintended consequences.

I have learned this lesson over and over. When I became a student of yoga, no one who knew me, neither my family nor my friends, had any idea what I was doing. For all they knew, I was sitting on nails every morning. I used to long for everyone to understand and practice yoga so I wouldn't feel so weird.

No doubt my wishes were inconsequential in their effect, nonetheless today, decades after I began my practice, yoga practice has indeed spread everywhere in the West. Unfortunately, the results of this popularity is that apparently what has spread the most widely tends to be the most superficial aspects of yoga.

Stop anyone on the street today with the question "what is yoga?" and they likely will tell you that yoga consists of challenging exercises done in heated rooms to lose weight and get fit.

I feel despair at this truth, but now find myself happily cheered by reading *Yoga: A Beginner's Guide*. The authors remind the reader that the power of yoga is so much greater than the limited power to touch our toes. Yoga can teach each of us to touch our soul as well, and how to become free at long last from the tyranny of our mind.

I was lucky enough to meet Georg Feuerstein when we served together on the Advisory Board of *Yoga Journal Magazine* many years ago. I was equally awed by his dedication to his practice and by the depth of his knowledge about this ancient art of yoga I love so well.

The awe soon turned to admiration and friendship. We continued this friendship electronically from afar. Georg never failed to promptly answer any question I put to him about an esoteric yoga term or "what exactly did that verse from Patanjali mean again?". Brenda extended the same warm connection to me.

As mentioned before, I am cheered from my despair about the popular misunderstandings surrounding yoga in our culture in part because of the publication of *Yoga: A Beginner's Guide.* This book makes such a cogent, concise and readable argument for us all to re-dedicate ourselves to the profound truths to be found in the midst of our practice. And it is clear the authors mean us to rededicate equally to practice on the mat, on the meditation cushion, and in our daily lives, busily interacting with real human beings.

Georg and Brenda write with the conviction that can only be born from their personal and mature practice of yoga. They write not only from their brains with knowledge and wisdom, but also from their hearts with love and devotion. This is a very rare combination.

I take great inspiration in the fact that we can read this book, and pass it on with confidence to students of all levels knowing it will improve their practice and lives.

Simply put, I like this book. I like the book's organization that presents the vastness of yoga teachings with just enough depth to be valuable and just enough breadth to be interesting. The reader is neither talked down to nor overwhelmed.

Another thing I like about *Yoga: A Beginner's Guide* is its approachable tone. When I read it, I feel more like I am in the Feuerstein's living room having a deep but personal conversation with like-minded friends.

I am especially appreciative of the *Questions* section at the end of the book. Yoga teachers are asked these kinds of questions all the time, and I for one am thrilled to have such an excellent guide to recommend.

ॐ

Finally, I cannot pass up the opportunity to state here how much I believe the world has lost when we lost Georg Feuerstein: an outstanding scholar, a fine friend and a devoted yogi. May the example of his life and the wisdom of his books remain with us forever.

Judith Hanson Lasater, Ph.D., PT
San Francisco, California
June, 2013

Judith Lasater has taught yoga since 1971. She holds a doctorate in East-West Psychology and is a physical therapist. She is president of the California Yoga Teachers Association and the author of eight books, including Relax and Renew; Yogabody; *and* Living Your Yoga.

PREFACE

Yoga was introduced in 1893 when the illustrious Swami Vivekananda, a yogi from India, spoke to an enthusiastic crowd of Westerners at the World's Parliament of Religions in Chicago. Since then literally thousands of books on Yoga have been published. Most of them treat Yoga as a system of body improvement in one way or another. We refer to that as "Modern Postural Yoga"—a phrase coined by the British scholar Elizabeth de Michelis (2004). Especially since the 1960s, with TV programs like Richard Hittleman's, millions of people in the Western hemisphere have taken up (and have significantly benefited from) this version of Yoga. Had they not experienced Yoga's beneficial effects, they would most certainly not have stuck with it year after year.

The majority of Yoga enthusiasts, especially in North America, are unfortunately ignorant of the fact that Yoga is very much more than physical postures for flexibility, fitness, strength, or relaxation. They also do not understand that, in its original form, Yoga could do them even greater good.

Yoga stands for *spiritual discipline*, as it was developed in India over thousands of years. This is the focus of our present book. *Yoga: A Beginner's Guide* aims to be as simple an introduction to the authentic eachings of Yoga as we can make it. To be sure, Yoga traditionally included physical postures, but this was just *one* aspect of practice. Mental discipline was counted as far more important. Some approaches didn't even include any physical exercises other than the discipline of sitting still for a long time in order to meditate.

Above all, Yoga traditionally was wrapped within a *spiritual* framework. Every single discipline had the purpose of helping the practitioner to grow toward inner (or spiritual) freedom. Modern Postural Yoga, by contrast, largely excludes any spiritual (or even ethical) consideration. Thus, contemporary practitioners in the Western hemisphere are often shortchanged. They are neither made aware of the real nature of Yoga nor encouraged to explore it.

The spiritual poverty of much of Western Yoga is due to the fact that all too many Yoga teachers jump into teaching after only the most rudimentary training. We would argue that they are therefore generally ill equipped for the huge responsibility to correctly instruct others. Often this extends even to the postural practices. We do not wish to deny that many, if not most, modern practitioners of the physical postures of Yoga are significantly helped by them. Many scientific studies prove this beyond doubt. Yet, the core power of Yoga—which is in its spiritual and ethical wisdom—remains untapped.

Toward the end of this book, we have given our answers to the most commonly asked questions. They are of course given from the perspective of traditional Yoga. While some of our answers may fall into a range of "unpopular" views when assessed within the contemporary Yoga marketplace, we have attempted to remain true to tradition as we know it.

Notes about Terms: To keep things as simple as possible, throughout the book we will use only the most important technical words in the Sanskrit language that are frequently used in Western Yoga centers and schools (see Appendix A). A male practitioner will be referred to as a *yogin* (in the nominative case: *yogi*); a female practitioner as a *yogini* (with a long *i* at the end). Most modern Western practitioners know these two terms but don't always use them.

Further Reading and Study: At the end of this book, Appendix B lists and briefly describes some of Georg's other, Yoga-related books in stepwise fashion, so that anyone wanting to explore Yoga further has a useful graduated guide.

Many of Georg's other books on Yoga were not written for novices. As we have learned, even his *Path of Yoga*, republished by Shambhala in revised form in 2012, presupposes too much for some readers. This is why we wrote the present book, which, we hope, is simple in language and argument. We offer it to beginning students so that they may begin their journey into Yoga on the right foot. We wish all our readers well.

—Georg Feuerstein and Brenda Feuerstein
Traditional Yoga Studies
www.traditionalyogastudies.com

PART ONE

Exploring the Tradition of Yoga

1. Introducing Yoga

Yoga evolved on the Indian subcontinent over the course of several millennia. Its physical exercises continue to be developed today, partly in response to the physical limitations and also the mental challenges (notably the lack of concentration) of modern people. The difference between now and then is this: In the past, Yoga was developed by accomplished masters who had a *spiritual* interest first and foremost. Today, imaginative Yoga instructors invent physical postures and styles that they think will benefit or excite their students. It is fair to say that by no means would all of these new-fangled approaches have passed the critical eye and wisdom of a master from long ago. What, one wonders, would such masters have made of *Hiphop Yoga, Disco Yoga, Nude Yoga, Nude Hot Yoga, Ganja (Marijuana) Yoga,* and so on? Our brains reel.

Since we will use the word "spiritual" often in this book, let us explain what we mean by it up front. "Spiritual" suggests a quality that relates to the luminous core of our being, however you may understand it or whatever you may call it. That core goes beyond language and the mind. Yet, it is not religious as commonly understood. Yoga as a whole also ought not to be equated with religion. It developed by trial and error on the part of thousands of practitioners. Its goal is inner freedom—which is freedom from the compulsions of our limited personality; above all, freedom from the habit of self-centeredness. Yoga wants us to become as transparent as glass, or as clear as a mountain lake on a windless day, so that we can be present in the world with wisdom and compassion.

Yoga's goal does not contradict the highest aspirations that a deeply religious and mystically-inclined person has. Yet, as we said before, Yoga is not a religion. It is not merely a philosophy either. It is a *discipline.* This is not a popular word in our time, because we have become accustomed to doing "our own thing" at our own leisure. But Yoga is not someone else's discipline to which we have to conform rigidly. It is essentially *self-discipline.*

Yoga comes wrapped in certain philosophical ideas or ideals. These may have a Hindu, Buddhist, or Jain flavor. Perhaps, one day, the West will have its own form of "spiritual" Yoga, which then can be expected to have its own distinct philosophical coloring. Whatever form Yoga will take, it will most certainly not be materialistic.

Some schools of Yoga, admittedly, have a stronger religious element than others. The main point, though, is that Yoga comprises many approaches. Each approach is tailored to a particular personality type—the thinker, the man (or woman) of action, the performer of rituals, the heart-oriented person, the individual who enjoys singing or chanting, and certainly the contemplative, as well as the person who has strong monastic tendencies.

Yoga comes in three basic *forms* depending on the culture with which it is most closely associated: the Hindu, the Jain, and the Buddhist. These three are *not* religions, as often thought. All three are associated with their own distinct language, alphabet, architecture, art, scripture, and social customs. In this book, we will focus exclusively on Hindu Yoga, which is best known in the West. Increasingly, though, Buddhist Yoga—especially in the form of Tibetan Buddhism—is becoming popular. The Dalai Lama, who is commonly seen as *the* spokesman for Tibetan Buddhism, has much to do with this success. This has been especially so since he was awarded the Nobel Peace Prize in 1989—a most remarkable accomplishment for the political and spiritual leader of a remote country whose takeover and suppression by the Chinese has been all but ignored in the West. We in the Western world seem to take liberally from Tibetan Buddhism, but seldom reciprocate.

Each *form* of Yoga has many *branches*, which in turn encompass many *lineages* or *schools*. Thus, Hindu Yoga has seven major branches: Raja-Yoga (the path of contemplation), Hatha-Yoga (the path of physical transformation), Jnana-Yoga (the path of knowledge), Karma-Yoga (the path of ego-free action), Bhakti-Yoga (the path of the heart), Mantra-Yoga (the path of mantric repetition), and Tantra-Yoga (the path of ritual). Each branch is represented in the West to one degree or another by various schools. The most widespread branch in our part of the world is Hatha-Yoga, which is virtually synonymous with postural practice.

In India, this branch is far more inclusive and shares the spiritual goal with all other branches of Yoga. It also includes meditation techniques, breath control, and mantra recitation.

Jnana-Yoga is rarely practiced in our part of the world, and if it is, this path is often reduced to spiritual *talk* rather than actual practice. Even rarer is the great path of Raja-Yoga with its eight "limbs," as codified in the *Yoga-Sutra* of Patanjali, the Indian sage of about 200 A.D. Still less common is Bhakti-Yoga, and hardly anyone is familiar with the actual practice of Karma-Yoga.

The most controversial branch is Tantra-Yoga, or simply Tantra, which in the Western world (and increasingly also in India) has become almost completely and misleadingly sexualized. Originally, however, Tantra was designed and practiced as an approach utilizing the transformative power of ritual and visualization. We will talk about each of these branches—and more—in this book.

Some religious practitioners may feel nervous when they hear about Hindu Yoga, primarily when they think of multiple gods (which are, however, more like the angels of their own faith) and "pagan" rituals. It's important to note that these belong to the *culture* of Hinduism and there is no need to adopt them when we practice Yoga.

Whatever religious or non-religious framework we adopt in order to pursue Yoga, we must base our practice on the principle of reality.

From the unreal lead me to the real,
from darkness lead me to light...

The above declaration is a guiding ideal expressed in a very old text written in the Sanskrit language—an ideal that Yoga embraces completely.

Yogic spirituality is about reality. If you can face reality, you will find traditional Yoga—which is spiritual discipline—meaningful. You can safely read on! If you have some preferred *version* of reality in your head onto which you wish to cling, then this is the point where you ought to either close this book or bravely and open-mindedly read on anyway.

2. The Secret of Change

We are subject to change from the moment we are conceived to the moment we die. We grow physically and mentally in the span of our life. If we are fortunate and take the initiative, we also grow spiritually.

Change is inside and around us. We cannot think of life without change. Yet, many people have a problem with change. When life is good to them, they want things to stay the same. When they encounter "bad" experiences, they want time to move rapidly ahead. Sitting nervously in the waiting room of a dentist's office is a classic example. Time seems to stand still, and we want the whole experience over and done with. This attitude is, however, quite unrealistic. The minutes click by as they will. We have control only over our internal sense of time, which is forged by the mind.

We can relate *consciously* to the inevitability of change and engage change as deliberate self-transformation. This lies in fact at the heart of all spiritual disciplines, including Yoga. Self-transformation means meeting life consciously, with wide-open eyes, and seeing it as an ever available opportunity to make positive changes in ourselves—from mastering our nicotine or alcohol addiction, to overcoming constant feelings of guilt or inadequacy, to becoming friendlier and more helpful toward others. The field of possible conscious change is wide open.

As spiritual practitioners, we work on ourselves not just because others want us to, or because we want to move ahead in life, but because we see the advantage in gaining control over our mind and destiny and becoming a benign presence in the world. When we have mastered our own mind, we are inwardly balanced and not subject to the whims of the ego. We are able to take into account the needs of others.

One idea in Yoga that is seldom mentioned by contemporary practitioners is that of benefiting the world. (Many modern Yoga practitioners seem too preoccupied with their own problems.) In the *Bhagavad-Gita* (3.20), a Sanskrit text from over 2,000 years ago, this idea is called *loka-samgraha,* which means something like "pulling together the world." We pull the world together by promoting the welfare of all. This can mean elevating the world socially or spiritually.

We think here of individuals like Mother Teresa and Mahatma Gandhi in India, or Martin Luther King and, before him, Hugh Burnett in North America. Each served people in his or her own way but always bearing the larger good in mind.

Mother Teresa, who died in 1997 at the age of eighty-seven, was a Catholic nun of Albanian descent and a Nobel laureate (1979). She chose to serve the poor, sick, and dying in Calcutta tirelessly for forty-five years.

Mohandas Karamchand Gandhi, better known as "Mahatma" (great soul) was an Indian national and a lawyer, who resisted British rule in India. He was at the center of the Indian independence movement and was assassinated in 1948 for his political convictions.

Martin Luther King, an African-American, was a Baptist minister and civil rights leader. He, too, was assassinated at the young age of thirty-nine. And he, too, received the Nobel Peace Prize in 1964. Following the example of Gandhi, he employed non-violent means to achieve his political goals.

Hugh Burnett was an African-Canadian who descended from slaves and, apart from working as a carpenter, was a dedicated civil rights leader. His carpentry business was boycotted when he stood up against racial discrimination, which had been abolished by law but was observed selectively in the Canadian province of Ontario.

In the *Bhagavad-Gita,* the enlightened master Krishna promoted the ideal of *loka-samgraha.* Although he supported the war between two tribes and their allies, his yogic teaching was designed to bring the people together and instil both peace and tranquility. The *Bhagavad-Gita* is a "must-read" along with the *Yoga-Sutra.* These two Sanskrit scriptures are in fact widely studied in Western Yoga circles.

3. The Mind: Agent of Change

Our culture places a premium on the mind. At the same time, however, we don't acknowledge the degree to which the mind shapes our destiny. Yet, this fact is easy to see. The mind allows us to interpret reality correctly or wrongly. We know from psychology that perception, which tells us how things are around us, is loaded with mental assumptions. Most of the time, we don't really see things as they are. We literally make things up or distort them. Often this doesn't matter. But sometimes it has grievous consequences for us and others.

We may dismiss, suppress, or even, as was the case with the German Nazis or the followers of Saddam Hussein, seek to exterminate an entire ethnic group. Or we may, based on our interpretation of reality, go to war and kill, or see no problem with mowing down virgin forests and allowing many species of plants and animals to become extinct. In an as yet unpublished manuscript, entitled *Empower Your Change,* we wrote:

> There is also the remarkable effect of the so-called placebo ("I shall please") effect, which is involved in all medical interventions. This is the curious "mind over matter" phenomenon, which leads to health improvement that cannot be explained by the medical or pharmacological intervention itself but depend on the patient's positive mindset. Thus, a fake knee surgery can improve or completely cure a serious knee problem. Or the kind attitude and verbal encouragement of the physician can work physical and psychological wonders. The placebo effect, which works in about 35% of cases, can last for months and even years.

Everything we know is filtered through the mind. As the placebo effect shows, this can be to our advantage. Often it is not.

The mind can also slay. It can hold us back. Spiritual ignorance is likely to give us the wrong picture of the world, which then prevents us from taking the first step on the spiritual path. Instead of moving toward inner freedom, we become more enmeshed in "unfreedom," or what is called "bondage."

Thus, having the right view is crucial. And the right view can be gleaned from the teachings of the great masters, who are spiritual experts. Our faith in experts shows that we value the opinions of those we believe to be in the know. We would do well to extend the same faith to the "opinions" of spiritual adepts. In fact, we should trust them more readily than we trust technical experts. The masters have nothing at stake, whereas an expert can be governed by self-interest, and often he or she is indeed self serving. Experts can be, and have been, hired to misinform the public. Witness the fiasco over whether smoking cigarettes damages health or not. The verdict has been out for some time. Hired experts and the industry were lying for years. This would not happen with the great masters; they can be relied upon to tell the truth.

Although spiritual teachings show considerable variation, they share a common ground of growth through wisdom. We can, therefore, trust them enough to launch our spiritual pilgrimage. The more we are able to suspend our preconceptions, predispositions, and emotional partialities, we will come to know reality. To know reality "as it is" is one of the objectives of Yoga.

For growth in Yoga to happen, we must understand our mind. When we use the word "self-knowledge," we refer to the workings of the mind. *Our* mind. Self-knowledge has the quality of wisdom, which is liberating.

4. Traditional Yoga Today

Yoga was invented and developed in the rural areas of India. Its social and cultural environment was starkly different from that of our own time. How, then, can Yoga be meaningful to us today? This is an all-important question, and we will attempt to answer it as clearly as we can.

Our lifestyles have become far more hectic than that of pre-modern India. We no longer allow ourselves the "luxury" of quietude. Most people live in overcrowded and horribly noisy and polluted cities with endless distractions. Our mentality has adjusted accordingly. We are restless, agitated, ambitious, distracted, and wanting to hoard ever more consumer goods while staying as comfortable and unchallenged as possible. But despite our luxurious lifestyle, true contentment escapes us.

At the same time, however, we are more dissatisfied and unhealthy than ever, and we hunger for a meaningful life. Other than this, it's difficult to see that humanity has changed significantly since the beginning of civilization. We certainly know more in terms of science, but our mind has not changed in fundamental ways from the time the sages of India formulated the principles of a sound and wholesome way of life. We are still suffering from anger, fear, greed, envy, jealousy, and all the other negative emotions that our ancestors suffered as well. We experience joy and sadness, pleasure and displeasure, contentment and grief, and so on. We have preferences, prejudices, preconceptions, likes and dislikes, as did our forebears long ago. For the most part, we still don't know how to deal with negative as well as positive mental states in a way that leads to balance, integration, and self acceptance. To be able to do so is one of the preliminary purposes of Yoga.

The teachings of Yoga can undoubtedly help at various levels—mind, body and spirit. How we use those teachings, however, is up to us. Some people settle exclusively on postural practice to trim their posteriors, stretch their tendons, or strengthen their muscles, while others enlist mantra practice or meditation to unwind and keep fit, or restore their health. A few employ Yoga for spiritual sustenance and inner growth.

Both Georg and I have taken up the path for essentially spiritual purposes, and have been grateful that we plunged into this venture when we were enthusiastic and idealistic, but still too young to really understand the depth of the commitment and sacrifices that would be expected of us. Over the decades, Yoga has been keeping us on the right track and definitely has helped us mature on the spiritual path. For many years, Georg stumbled along in his Yoga practice and understanding, but periodically a kind-hearted teacher would show up to help him out of a dead end of his own making and point him in the right direction again. Brenda found her teacher later in life. Gradually, the path has become clearer for us, and the stumbling has become more subtle. But spiritual life is necessarily a learning experience, an uphill path. It is just that we become more capable of adjusting to the rarefied air of the higher ranges of the climb.

To engage Yoga properly, we must be willing to embrace life-positive change. Even if all you desire from Yoga is to trim and strengthen your body, this implies you want to change (change your physical body, that is). If you want to employ Yoga to settle your emotions or balance your mind, you must be willing to transform your mind. This is not easy. Self-transformation is challenging and inconvenient. It calls for attentive self-discipline 24/7 and a basic willingness to explore yourself—even the dark niches of your mind.

But anyone who values knowledge in the form of self-knowledge will not reject adherence to this difficult path. Several years ago, Georg came up with Twelve Steps to explain this side of Yoga, which we want to share in a modified version in the next chapter.

5. The Twelve Steps of Spiritual Recovery

The following Twelve Steps, rephrased for our purposes here, are modeled after the AA program, which nowadays is widely used for all sorts of addictions—from nicotine to alcohol to sex, and more.

1. *We admit* the fact that we live our ordinary life only half awake, in something of a trance state, and that we normally deny this to ourselves.

2. *We begin to look and ask for guidance* in our effort to cultivate a new attitude of wakefulness. This means seeking out supportive people (such as those at a good Yoga center) and choosing uplifting reading material.

3. *We initiate positive changes* in our behavior, which affirm that new attitude, or outlook. It is not enough to read and talk about spiritual principles. We need to make our spirituality eminently practical by committing to a daily routine and an appropriate lifestyle.

4. *We practice self-understanding*; that is, we accept conscious responsibility for noticing our automatic (trance-like) programs and where they fall short of our new understanding of life.

5. *We make a commitment to undergo the purification* necessary to change our old mental and emotional patterns and stabilize the new outlook and disposition.

6. *We learn to be flexible* and open to life, so that we can continue to learn and grow on the basis of our new outlook. Openness should never be indiscriminate but be based on proper discernment.

7. *We practice humility* in the midst of our endeavors to mature spiritually. In this way we avoid the danger of ego inflation.

8. *We assume responsibility* for what we have understood about life and the principles of spiritual recovery, applying our understanding to all our relationships, so that we can be a benign influence in the world.

9. Guided by our new outlook and with the help of Yoga, *we work on the integration* of our mind.

10. *We conscientiously cultivate self-discipline* in all matters, great and small. This can be painstaking and inconvenient at times because we will be looking at our actions more closely on a ongoing basis.

11. *We increasingly practice* spiritual communion with the luminous part of ourselves through a regular meditation practice. Through this and through continued growth in self-understanding, we become gradually transparent to ourselves.

12. *We open ourselves* to the possibility of abiding happiness whereby self-centeredness is cleared away and we recover our true spiritual essence, which had been covered over. Through this awakening, the world becomes transparent to us, and we are made whole in the context of life.

Each branch of Yoga has its own version of the path. We will explain this shortly. But first we want to turn to an existential matter with which we are all too familiar but which, generally, we like to ignore: the fact of suffering.

6. Suffering Beyond Pain

We scrape our skin falling, and there is pain. We bump hard into a corner, and there is considerable pain. We have a hole in a tooth, and awful pain wells up, and when painkillers stop working, we finally run to the dentist. We break our arm, and there is excruciating pain. And so on. We can be certain that in the course of our life, even the healthiest person will experience pain occasionally.

As long as we are unenlightened, all of us experience suffering without fail. The enlightened can experience pain but have conquered suffering. So, what is suffering? Suffering is the kind of mental distress associated with pain—anger, animosity, grief, fear, anguish, sorrow, frustration, jealousy, envy, doubt, distrust, suspicion, resentment, bitterness. To give some practical examples: Suffering is when we find a bruise somewhere on our body for which we have no immediate explanation, and our mind fearfully drifts right away to thoughts of cancer. Or we have to sit for an academic test but feel utterly unprepared and worry about the result. Or we are painfully shy and dread being in large groups. Or our dreams are filled with unpleasant imagery. Or we mull over past bad experiences or anticipate them in the future. Or we have to put up with noise in the neighborhood, icy temperatures in winter and soaring temperatures in summer. Or we are forced to work at a job we find boring or stressful. Or, perhaps, we have to be around people we don't like or are obliged to be away from those we love.

Whether we experience pain or not, our life is full of suffering. Most of us remain blind to this fact and imagine that we have a "pretty good" life. We indulge in this fantasy until, suddenly, our life is interrupted by a major tragedy that stops us in our tracks. The greatest suffering is associated with death—the actual demise of a loved person or our own approaching death, which we fear.

The cause of suffering is the sense of "I," which refers both pleasant and unpleasant life experiences to itself. Suffering does not happen in the absence of the ego. Thus, an enlightened master may have physical pain but no suffering, because he or she has transcended the ego. He or she does not mull over his fate only because the body is aching or ailing. He or she does not overinterpret, or mentalize, the painful experiences of life. Pain is simply pain—a sense experience that is of little consequence.

For a spiritual seeker, who may have become somewhat aware and therefore sensitized, life may hold more of the quality of suffering than for the ordinary person, who is vital and steamrolls through with little awareness. The same is comparatively true with other species. For example, a bin full of worms that feed on and break down compost can probably experience pain but, as far as one can tell, they don't suffer. Your dog, however, does appear to suffer when he is denied more food. He may even look quite dejected. But the moment he is offered a bone or dog cookie, his eyes may noticeably brighten in an instant. And certainly one can witness various suffering-reactions in children. On a gloomy, rainy day, many children don't want to play outdoors and may look quite miserable, but the moment you tell them that there are cookies available, they suddenly cheer up.

The problem is that even positive experiences are potentially full of suffering—ponder the fact that a good experience will not last forever or that someone has a better experience than we do, and a subtle form of suffering starts. Or consider a child overwhelmed with choosing what they would like for a birthday or Christmas gift; the gifts seem to agitate the child's mind. Or think of an adult's reaction when he or she is presented with a gift that is less than expected. Disappointment is suffering, too.

The best medicine for suffering is equanimity, or inner calm. When we cultivate an even-tempered, balanced mind, we are immunizing ourselves against the mood of suffering. We just don't add suffering on top of pain or on top of some trauma. Instead, we are able to meet things as they are. A mole on your skin is not inevitably future cancer. Present cancer is not inevitably certain death. And so on. In equanimity, we don't unnecessarily elaborate. We don't let fear dominate our thinking. We don't fantasize or even neurotically project ahead.

Entire industries get rich on our anxieties: We are too fat, too unfit, too drab, too "uncool," too ignorant, etc. So, we set out to improve ourselves. But the efforts we must make to fit some imaginary ideal are formidable. They amount to a pointless struggle.

Once upon a time, for example, being fat was the norm. Think of the Venus of Willendorf from the Stone Age! Then later, the cultural norm of "beauty" was having a wasp-like waist. At another time in history long dresses were in, only to be replaced decades later by the mini. Attempting to keep up with fashion styles becomes insane, because soon the fashion industry is controlling your mind.

Yoga is not about mere self-improvement, as normally understood. It focuses on real change, or self-transformation. If you want to strive, does it not make sense to struggle for something worthwhile?

Because Indian thought considers suffering to be a fundamental fact of life, Indian philosophy has often been deemed pessimistic by those who lacked a more thorough knowledge of its principles. What could be more positive than the ideal of spiritual freedom? As we will see, this ideal is written even into the value pyramid of Hinduism, which has liberation as its apex. The thought that we *can* overcome suffering is entirely optimistic. Yoga is essentially an optimistic path that puts the controls in your hands.

7. Raja-Yoga: The Path of Contemplation

The royal (*raja*) road of Yoga is intended for advanced practitioners. We mention this branch of Hindu Yoga up front because of its connection with the postural practice.

Raja-Yoga goes back to a sage named Patanjali—a name that is often heard in Yoga centers. He wrote a Sanskrit text called the *Yoga-Sutra*. (Many people say "*Yoga-Sutras*", because this work consists of 195 aphorisms, or *sutras*, on Yoga.) As with other Yoga authorities, Patanjali`s lifetime is not known precisely, but most scholars place him in the second century C.E.

His eightfold version of the yogic path consists of:

1. Moral disciplines (*yama*)
2. Self-restraint (*niyama*)
3. Postures (*asana*)
4. Breath control (*pranayama*)
5. Withdrawal of the senses (*pratyahara*)
6. Concentration (*dharana*)
7. Meditation (*dhyana*)
8. Ecstasy (*samadhi*)

As you can see, postural practice, which is the focus of much of modern Yoga, is really only the third step, or "limb." It is preceded by two very important sets of practices, which are generally ignored by the "mainstream" of modern Yoga. Practitioners who are respectful of the Yoga tradition would argue that without the inclusion of the moral disciplines, we should not expect to grow spiritually. In other words, the *yamas* need to be observed in some form or another to engage Yoga as a spiritual discipline. While these first two limbs are part of some Yoga teacher training programs, by no means are they present in all.

The moral disciplines of Yoga are basic moral values, which are found in all major religions of the world and can be endorsed by any sane person, whether of a religious or secular bent of mind.

According to Patanjali, the moral disciplines include the following five observances, which should be heeded under any circumstance and at all times: nonharming, truthfulness, nonstealing, chastity, and freedom from greed.

How is this different from religious commandments, you might ask? There is indeed a decisive difference. Yoga does not stipulate moral norms that we must obey to avoid divine punishment or win approval. The above-cited moral values—and others mentioned in other Yoga texts—are meant to simply regulate our social behavior, so that our spiritual endeavors can bear fruit.

One of the objections to Yoga by certain religious sects is that God is left out of consideration in all this, and that Yoga masters act under their own power. We would argue that such an assertion makes two unwarranted assumptions, namely that Yoga masters are necessarily godless or God-defying, and that a sensible moral provision means nothing unless God has sanctioned it.

Yama: The Five Moral Disciplines

1. We all can accept that nonharming—often called non-violence—is a sound principle. A society that allows harming others at will—a bit like movie portrayals of the Wild West—could not really function constructively; nor could a society that glorifies or allows lying and stealing. In our contemporary culture, matters are less clear when it comes to chastity and freedom from greed.

Nonharming (*ahimsa*) is extensive. Patanjali tells us that it happens physically, mentally, and also in speech. We recommend that a beginning Yoga student spends a fair amount of time considering *how* he or she might harm others—not just fellow humans but all beings, however miniscule and seemingly insignificant.

Such a serious consideration may well have repercussions in almost every area of your life, including: your choice of foods—such as whether these will include animal products, or fruits and vegetables that have been sprayed with pesticides, etc; your treatment of animals; your choices of entertainment for yourself and your children (like TV, or circus or zoo); your use of transportation that encourages environmental pollution; your support (or non-support) of political activities or social causes—like invasion, war, poverty.

2. *Untruthfulness* has many forms. We practice it when we lie about our age or some other personal detail. Some instances may seem insignificant and some we excuse by saying that "everybody does it." We speak of "insincerity," "misrepresentation" or "making a mistake" in order to soften the implications of the word "lying." But it is still dishonest.

3. Similarly *theft* (stealing) is widespread in our society and ranges from cheating on our taxes to accepting wrong change when it is in our favor. Could over-consumption be considered theft? Do we steal from the have-nots? And on and on.

4. About *chastity...* Patanjali was obviously an ascetic and wrote for ascetics who were dedicated to full-time Yoga practice. As an ascetic, he thought that abstention from sex was the best policy, and he didn't allow any wiggle room on this. But we know that for thousands of years, Yoga has included both ascetics and lay practitioners. Lay practitioners meant people who were married and had families; therefore, individuals who also engaged in sex. Since the contemporary Yoga movement consists almost entirely of lay folk, it is important to understand what *chastity* might mean in their case. Scriptures other than Patanjali's *Yoga-Sutra,* which was composed for hardcore ascetics, help us out on this point: For lay people, chastity means *disciplined* sexual activity. While we ought not to repress our sexual drive, we should also not simply indulge it at our whim. Mature self-inquiry will help us determine the best course in such matters, which must consider biological urge, consent, emotion, the role of the mind, and the situation.

5. *Freedom from greed* is not an easy consideration either, because greed is rampant in our contemporary society, which grossly over-consumes and socializes our children to start this unfortunate habit as early as possible. Georg has written at length about this vice and many others in his hard-hitting book *Yoga Morality,* which you might want to read down the road. For a beginning Yoga student, it is enough to know—if you don't know it already—that greed is involved in many of our modern habits and the destruction of the natural environment.

Georg and I have written about the environmental devastation and the role Yoga can play in creating a saner society, with an interest in restoring the health of our ailing environment. We address Hindu Yoga in our book *Green Yoga* (2007) and Buddhist Yoga in *Green Dharma* (2008), which is available on our website as an ebook at *www.traditionalyogastudies.com.*

Niyama

The second step of Patanjali's eightfold path is self-restraint (*niyama*). He understands this as having five components: purity, contentment, asceticism, study, and dedication to the lord.

Purity includes both physical and mental purity, and various schools of Yoga offer a wide range of purification exercises. *Contentment*—a rare virtue nowadays—is feeling satisfied with what one has. *Asceticism*, which may raise hackles in today's readers, is essentially an attitude of disciplining the body and the mind. Patanjali is very clear that this practice should not be a form of self-inflicted torture but be all-round beneficial. *Study* stands for immersing oneself in the wisdom of Yoga, so that we gain understanding as well as proper motivation.

The last practice of self-restraint is *dedication to the lord*, which is often interpreted as devotion to God. But, in Yoga, "the lord" is considered one among countless spiritual Selves, and so the term "God" is not entirely applicable, although we can understand it in this way. Certainly, contemporary practitioners who already have made a religious commitment can take this virtue to mean simply dedication to a spiritual ideal.

Asana

We need not say much about *asana*: *posture*, the third step, because this practice is prominent in almost every Western Yoga center. For Patanjali, it still meant no more than the most convenient posture for meditation. He did not even mention the health benefits from postural practice that are emphasized today.

Pranayama

Breath control is conscious control over the otherwise automatic function of breathing. Yoga masters discovered early on that the breath and the mind are intimately linked and that by carefully regulating the breathing rhythm, we can effectively calm the mind.

Pratyahara

Sense-withdrawal—sometimes referred to as sensory inhibition—is control over our sensory functions, so that the senses (sight, hearing, smell, taste, and touch) do not carry our attention away at random. Sometimes we become totally absorbed in meditating upon a chosen object, that is, we are unaware of what is going on in the outside world.

Dharana

Concentration is sustained focusing of the mind in preparation of meditation.

Dhyana

Meditation is allowing the mind to dwell in a relaxed and almost effortless manner on the selected object of concentration.

Samadhi

When it occurs, *ecstasy* happens spontaneously by growing out of sustained meditation. The essence of ecstasy consists in a seamless merging with the object of meditation. If your object of meditation is, for instance, the thought of your pet dog, you experience becoming one with your dog. If your object is something more elevated, you find yourself at one with it too. This is an extraordinary experience, which is generally accompanied by an overwhelming feeling of ease and happiness. Little wonder that many people confuse ecstasy with freedom. An unexpectedly large number of people experience ecstasy or ecstasy-like states without the least preparation and without taking psychedelic drugs. Often, they benefit from such states, but sometimes they are just confused by them. It is clearly better to be prepared for this eventuality by the systematic practice of Yoga.

It is important to realize that ecstasy is *not* the end of the yogic journey. Rather, the grand goal is spiritual liberation, which is also called "enlightenment." This is not merely a temporary experience but a state of being that cannot be lost. It is who you are!

ॐ

As you can appreciate, the eight steps mapped out by Patanjali do not fulfill themselves overnight. Success in Yoga comes with dedicated *lifelong* practice. Anyone promising "enlightenment" in a weekend, or even as a "sure thing," is plainly a charlatan. Save yourself the expense and settle down to practicing Yoga step by careful step.

Georg took his first baby steps in Yoga at the age of thirteen and, after fifty years of practice, he still did not claim to be enlightened. Some told him that he had become more compassionate. If true, he was happy, because for him compassion counted for a lot more than the ability to meditate, recite complicated mantras, spout Sanskrit quotations, or go into ecstasy at the drop of a hat. Brenda started with Yoga postures as a young child when she was practicing along with Kareen Zebroff on TV. Later on, she taught Yoga for many years in Saskatchewan and gradually also became aware of the spirituality of Yoga. Like Georg, she also cannot claim to have become enlightened, though people think she is a compassionate person.

What we both *could* claim, however, is that we have learned a lot about ourselves and have become clear about the path and clear about the spiritual goal. And that, in turn, deepened our commitment to continue in Yoga, transforming ourselves more and more, becoming clearer vehicles for shining forth the light at the heart of all beings.

8. Hatha-Yoga: The Path of Physical Transformation

Hatha Yoga is assumed to be the most widely practiced Yoga in the West. But, really, there is a big difference between contemporary efforts going by the name of "Hatha-Yoga" and traditional Hatha-Yoga, as it emerged in India perhaps a thousand years ago. *Hatha* means force, and Hatha-Yoga has been correctly translated as "Forceful Yoga." But, as we will explain shortly, the word *hatha* also has a hidden, or esoteric, meaning.

When we examine the medieval Sanskrit texts on Hatha-Yoga, we find that this branch of Yoga is not just about postures, as widely taught in the West. Traditional Hatha-Yoga really offers a full path all its own, which is not unlike the eightfold path of Raja-Yoga. It features ethical considerations (though they are not always listed as a separate category) and aims at the lofty ideal of spiritual freedom. Although its repertoire includes many postures, so-called "seals" and "locks," Hatha-Yoga primarily revolves around the control of the breath and the mind. "Seals" are postures that hold the energy within the body, and the three types of "locks" are maneuvers that have essentially the same purpose.

Hatha-Yoga also has a good many purification practices, including diet. These are rarely to be found in contemporary Hatha-Yoga. Yet, in any type of traditional Yoga, for instance, diet is decisive, and an organic vegetarian diet is preferred for health and ethical reasons. More and more Western physicians are telling us the same, because most beef is shot through with bovine growth hormones and antibiotics, and fish is full of mercury because of the increasing pollution of the oceans, lakes, and rivers. For a Yoga practitioner, there is also the vital issue of the well-documented brutality involved in raising livestock.

Having said this, we also acknowledge that vegetarianism is not possible for everyone. There are regions in the world where it is simply not possible to grow or obtain vegetables, and where we (the authors) must practice nonharming in the form of tolerance.

The high art of meditation, which is integral to the practice of Hatha-Yoga, is pursued as a kind of visualization; and enlightenment—the supreme goal—is understood as a matter of totally transforming the physical body into a body of light. Historically, Hatha-Yoga was closely connected with alchemy and regarded the body as an alchemical cauldron in which the *yogin* skillfully mixed the body's energies.

From Tantra, Hatha-Yoga inherited the notion that consciousness has an energetic aspect. These two interrelated realities (consciousness and energy) are in actuality undivided. In the ordinary person, however, they are polarized in the body. Consciousness is associated with the crown of the head and the energetic aspect is located in potential form at the base of the spine. This energy must be activated, or "awakened," and conducted along the body's central axis to the crown, where it merges with consciousness. This merging yields a high state of ecstasy.

This energy is known as the "coiled power," "serpent power," or *kundalini.* When the energy at the base is carefully led up to the crown mainly by means of breath control and concentration, the resulting state of ecstasy takes the *yogin* beyond the brain-dependent mind. Since the *kundalini* energy tends to sink back to a dormant state at the base of the spine, it must be activated and returned to the crown over and over again. When this is done, the whole body becomes transformed into a body of light. This is not just meant symbolically. There are many stories of *yogins* actually accomplishing this feat, the most famous being Ramalinga Swami of South India in the twentieth century. The "body of light" is known in various religio-spiritual traditions around the world, including Christianity, where it is known among mystics as the "resurrection body" or the "body of glory."

The polarity between consciousness and its energetic aspect is associated with the seven (or more) energetic centers called *cakras,* which, "like blossoms on a stem," are aligned along the spinal column and correspond (but are *not* identical with) the nerve plexuses. The most important center is located at the crown of the head, the place of consciousness, which is the focus of many meditation techniques.

The awakening of the *kundalinī* energy is brought about by the union of two energetic currents—esoterically called "sun" (represented by the syllable *ha*) and "moon" (represented by the syllable *tha*). Many people think that these two syllables *mean* "sun" and "moon," but this is incorrect. The former current is connected with the breath flowing through the right nostril and the latter with the breath flowing through the left nostril. But the combination of the two currents gives us the hidden meaning of the word *hatha* (pronounced "hut-ha"!), as indicated earlier.

9. Jnana-Yoga: The Path of Knowledge

This branch of Yoga is at the heart of a tradition called "Vedanta," which was first taught in the ancient *Upanishads* (esoteric Sanskrit texts that were originally taught by word of mouth only). Jnana-Yoga was formulated almost in opposition to the old Indian school of ritualism. It put forward knowledge (*jnana*), or wisdom, as the means to inner freedom. The knowledge in question is *not* conventional or scientific knowledge but insight into the difference between the real and the unreal (false or illusory). The real is said to lead us to inner freedom, while the unreal keeps us entrapped in all the many things that distract us from finding out who we truly are beyond the name or religious affiliation given to us at birth, the occupation by which we earn our livelihood, the political membership we have chosen, and so on.

Jnana-Yoga is based on the understanding that all the countless things we perceive are in reality one. This is a difficult concept to comprehend. People who have experimented with psychedelic drugs have an easier time to understand this, which is not to say that we recommend such drugs. There are states of consciousness in which the distinction between the experiencer (i.e., you) and the experienced world is lifted. Subject and object are merged. Now, according to Jnana-Yoga, the ultimate realization, or spiritual liberation, is *not* merely an experience; it is not a mental state that can be acquired or lost. Spiritual liberation *is* reality. And reality is forever. Normally, what we see as reality (i.e., our personality and the world) is really a product of the *un*enlightened mind. Our experience of separate things (a tree, a mountain, a lake, etc.) is illusory. The sense of "I" is also illusory. We mysteriously identify with a particular ("our") mind and a particular ("our") body. In truth, we are the Self. Everyone is the same Self. Everyone is the same essence of the world. Beyond, behind, or beneath the multitude of forms is one Supreme Identity, and we are all that One.

A classic illustration of this unity is this: An empty earthen pot (our body-mind) is surrounded by space (the Self). The same space also exists inside the pot. When the pot is shattered (i.e., when the body-mind dies), the inner and outer space continues as before.

Jnana-Yoga revolves around the recognition that our innermost essence, the Self (*atman*), is really beyond the mind. Moreover, that Self is also the essence of the world (*brahman*). Thus we get the fundamental formula: *atman* = *brahman*.

In some works, the path of Jnana-Yoga consisted of three aspects: (1) listening carefully to the oral instructions of one's teacher; (2) pondering the metaphysical truths received from one's teacher, and (3) meditating deeply on those truths until the Self is realized. The *yogin* of this path endeavours to be constantly mindful of the truth that there is only one reality.

In the fifteenth century, the path of Jnana-Yoga was elaborated in the *Vedanta-Sara* ("Essence of Vedanta") to comprise four principal means: (1) discernment (*viveka*) between the real and the unreal; (2) renunciation of whatever reward may derive from one's activities; (3) the "six accomplishments" consisting of tranquillity, restraint of one's senses, abstention from irrelevant activity, patience, mental concentration, and faith (which we may interpret as a positive attitude to life), and (4) the urge toward liberation, or enlightenment.

This is a demanding spiritual path, which calls for great mental clarity, integrity, and staying power. Otherwise it remains at the level of an intellectual game. It is not enough to affirm "I am That"—a common mantra or significator of non-duality used by practitioners of this way. We must also *feel this deeply* and, above all, realize or *be* this. By extension, we must live that way. Jnana-Yoga is often said to be particularly suited for intellectuals. In our experience, this is not so. Intellectuals tend to intellectualize everything, including Yoga. This, the Sanskrit sources tell us, will not get us very far; certainly not to freedom.

It may be more correct to call Jnana-Yoga the path of wisdom rather than knowledge. (The term *jnana* can mean either "knowledge" or "wisdom" and has been translated in a yogic context in both ways.) Many people today understand "knowledge," which is about information. But "wisdom" is something else. It has a living quality and can affect our life directly, in a significant way. Knowledge, on the other hand, can at times be worthless information. So, as you approach the path of Jnana-Yoga make sure you don't confuse the two but stick with life-transforming wisdom.

10. Karma-Yoga: The Path of Ego-Free Action

Raja-Yoga and Jnana-Yoga are obviously demanding approaches. Not everyone is capable of pursuing them. But the Yoga tradition also includes less challenging paths. One of them is Karma-Yoga, which was first formulated in the *Bhagavad-Gita* a little over 2,000 years ago. *Karma* (or *karman,* which is the grammatical stem) means literally "action." In the West, we generally understand this word "karma" in the sense of "destiny." The connection between action and destiny is this: All self-centered action has far-reaching consequences. That kind of action keeps us "bound," that is, it reinforces our state of "unenlightenment," or "un-wisdom."

Karma-Yoga is based on the recognition that to be alive means to be active. We cannot avoid all action. Our eyes see, our ears hear, our brain sends signals to every part of the body, and our lungs breathe. The Hindu sages realized that it is impossible to fulfill the ancient ideal of renouncing the world completely. Even when we decide to live in a remote mountain cave or a jungle, we cannot avoid all action. At the very least, we must feed our body to prevent disease and death.

The idea behind Karma-Yoga, then, is very simple: Cultivate only actions that are *not* self-centered and also are appropriate in the largest sense of the term. Self-centeredness is understood broadly as (1) acting from an unenlightened (and therefore inevitably egoic) perspective, (2) having selfish motives, and (3) hoping consciously or unconsciously for a reward or personal benefit.

What is appropriate action? Generally speaking, this is activity that maintains your or someone else's existence (eating, drinking, sleeping, keeping warm, etc.), or that fulfills one's accepted roles or tasks (such as parenting or being a responsible worker), and so on. This is not considered selfish in the sense of self-centered. The best activity focuses on your own and others' material, moral, mental, and spiritual welfare, *but* without getting the ego involved.

There are numerous people who do good in the world, who may even be called "saints." Yet, if there is the least shred of selfish motivation or expectation in their noble activity, they cannot be called *karma-yogins.* Selfish motivation is difficult to determine, because some of our seemingly blameless motivations have less respectable undercurrents. For instance, we may engage in charitable work because this gives *us* joy or because we "inherited" a humanitarian tendency from a parent, or because we want to favor a particular group with which we emotionally identify (like "our" sports team). Thus, even Karma-Yoga entails a good deal of subtle self-inspection (or discernment). It is, then, simple in theory but not necessarily in practice.

In our own era, an important aspect of Karma-Yoga concerns our natural environment. The ecosystem is at the brink of collapse—50,000 animal and plant species become extinct every year! This is uniquely different from the past, and so we also must find new ways of responding to the natural catastrophe around us. We are called to make our Karma-Yoga relevant to the world at large. We have discussed this at some length in our book *Green Yoga* (mainly for Hindu *yogins* and *yoginis*) and *Green Dharma* (primarily but not exclusively for Buddhist *yogins* and *yoginis*).

Specifically, we are challenged to come up with ways to reduce our personal impact on the environment ("our footprint"). Such challenges may include not driving so much or flying only when absolutely necessary, or not over-consuming while others are literally starving from hunger, or using up water while others have only dirty water to drink, and so on. These are undoubtedly challenging measures. But a *karma-yogin* or *-yogini* does what he or she can do to reduce the suffering of others, regardless of where these others live in the world.

Our Karma-Yoga, then, can be all-embracing and as broad as the world itself.

11. Bhakti-Yoga: The Path of the Heart

This is the most "religious" branch of Yoga, which involves belief in a personal deity, who is the one absolute reality. *Bhakti* means "devotion," which is often understood in the sense of "love." Thus the *Bhagavad-Gita,* which also gave us Karma-Yoga, taught that the devotional path is the highest. The one reality was called Vishnu ("Pervasive one"), who was thought to have had many divine incarnations (*avatara*), such as Krishna and Rama, but also incarnations as nonhuman beings. (Other "schools"–lines of transmission from teacher to student within the various branches of Yoga—place God Shiva or Goddess Shri at the head of creation as the ultimate Divine.)

Well known texts of the *bhakti* approach are the two *Bhakti-Sutras* and also a massive work called the *Bhagavata-Purana,* which focuses on Krishna. Westerners have become familiar with Krishna and Krishna devotion through the Krishna Consciousness movement, which goes back to a *bhakti* master of the late-fifteenth to early-sixteenth century.

Bhakti-Yoga involves typical religious practices, such as worship, chanting songs in praise of the Divine, prostrations in front of an image of God, telling and listening to edifying stories about God, and so on. A very common practice is recitation (*japa*) of the name of God, which is a means to bring the mind closer to God. All these practices have their relative equivalents in other faith traditions. We should, therefore, regard them with respect.

On the *bhakti* path, the devotee is encouraged to feel a growing passion for the Divine. This passion is deemed yogically legitimate, as it is free from self-centeredness. It culminates in a condition in which the *yogin* or *yogini* enters the immediate presence of the Divine. This is understood as "supreme devotion."

Many Westerners who already have a commitment to Christianity or Judaism, for example, may not be immediately attracted to Hindu Bhakti-Yoga. Many others, like those who have left behind all ritual expressions from the traditions into which they were born, may react strongly against religious beliefs and practices of any kind. Therefore, Bhakti-Yoga may be the least likely Yoga path for a Western-educated person to follow. Yet, some Yoga centers have images of Hindu deities, notably the elephant-headed Ganesha, who is understood as a remover of obstacles. We need not feel compelled to worship Ganesha or any other Hindu deity but can simply regard them as symbols of everyone's true spiritual potential.

Of course, some Westerners—who have become alienated from their early religious roots—find Bhakti-Yoga attractive even without joining a sect or traditional lineage. What is found attractive is that Bhakti-Yoga addresses the heart. This is not as outlandish as it sounds. As researchers have discovered, the heart is an important nervous center and has billions of neurons, which make it intelligent. The heart and the brain undoubtedly have to work together to produce a balanced human being. Even the most fervent Jnana-Yoga practitioner must have some quality of devotion or love to succeed on his or her path.

12. Mantra-Yoga: The Path of Potent Sound

Another technically easy path is Mantra-Yoga. This approach most often consists primarily in the more or less constant recitation of a *mantra* (a potent sound), such as *om,* or a longer phrase, such as *shivo'ham* (literally, "I am Shiva"), which actually means "I am the one reality." Alternatively, Mantra-Yoga encompasses a more complex path, comprised of sixteen "limbs." These limbs include posture, controlled breathing, concentration, meditation, ecstasy, and a range of ritual practices.

We will discuss here only the repetition of a *mantra*, which has become a very popular practice among Western students of Yoga. This Sanskrit word, *mantra,* which has entered our English dictionaries, is explained as "that which protects the mind." A *mantra* protects the mind by keeping it focused on the spiritual process, instead of allowing it to wander from thought to thought, or flit from experience to experience. Outside of meditation, it is notoriously difficult to be mindful, and we tend to get lost in automatic (unconscious) thinking, which is unproductive.

Mindful (attentive) recitation of a *mantra* can be done aloud, whispered, or even recited mentally. Beginners would do well to repeat their chosen *mantra* out loud, or at least whispered. Later on, they can switch to mental recitation. Recitation of a *mantra* so that you yourself can hear it has the advantage of giving you feedback through the ears. Then, when you stop your recitation, or find that you are mispronouncing it or saying it completely without any attention, you will become aware of this more quickly. Mental recitation does not have the same feedback, and you can get lost in thought (that is, go semi-conscious) far more readily.

The popular *mantra "om"* stands for the ultimate reality, however it may be conceived. You can conceive it as representing the ultimate nameless reality, the Godhead, or the Supreme Self. The main idea behind it is that there is something greater than you. The *om* (or *aum*) sound, by the way, has no *literal* meaning.

Ordinarily, a *mantra* is given by one's spiritual teacher. But, short of this, you can use whatever sound is meaningful to you. Of course, it would be undesirable to adopt a *mantra* that has spiritually negative or questionable connotations, such as "enmity" or "$E = mc^2$," or "I will succeed in my business." A *mantra* is supposed to help in your *spiritual* unfolding.

The biggest hurdle on the mantric path is boredom and the dullness of semi-consciousness. This is also a major obstacle in the practice of meditation. The mind, especially in modern times, expects to be constantly entertained. It wants distraction. So, when boredom sets in, it is best to remind oneself why one is practicing Yoga at all. We want to master the mind so that it does not blindly follow the senses, which give us any number of sensations that we then pursue: the television program, gossip, advertising billboard, or unnecessary and distracting information.

Normally, we allow the mind to do as it will. In Yoga, we seek to enlist it for the spiritual work. As the *Amrita-Bindu-Upanishad* (2) reminds us:

> The mind alone is the cause of bondage and liberation for humans. Attached to objects, (it leads) to bondage; freed from objects, it is said (to lead) to liberation.

13. Tantra-Yoga: The Path of Continuity

Tantra is the most difficult branch of Yoga, which we also describe as "the path of ritual," because rituals play an important part in most schools of Tantra. But the essential aspect of this approach is found in the Sanskrit term *tantra* itself, which means something like "continuity." What is implied in this is that Tantra-Yoga has at its center the recognition that there is no split between the ultimate reality and our ordinary reality. These are thought to be one and the same, although we experience them as radically distinct. All depends on one's perspective or state of consciousness. An enlightened adept sees the world as the one reality, whereas an unenlightened person views the world as unenlightened and regards the one reality as a goal in some other realm or future time.

"Continuity" means that the liberation—or "heaven"—to which we aspire is *here and now*. It is just that our unenlightened mind prefers to look upon the world as made up of so many good or bad things, people, or experiences. Then we struggle to realize liberation, the Self, or God beyond this world, thereby setting up a false dualism.

Tantra emerged about 500 C.E. and culminated about five centuries later. It was widely disseminated throughout India and has thousands of primary and secondary texts of which a small percentage is still available. The primary texts also bear the name *Tantra.*

Tantra's success was partly due to the fact that it presented itself as a new revelation meant for the "dark age" of the present era of the world. According to this teaching, there are four world ages that appear in cyclic fashion: a golden age in which spiritual values are foremost; a second world age in which spirituality is somewhat dimmer; a third world age, which involves a further physical, moral, and mental deterioration, and then the dark age in which ignorance, delusion, and especially the negative emotion of greed reign supreme. The last-mentioned world age reminds one of our own era. Spiritual practice, consisting above all in the mental discipline of mindfulness is particularly difficult in the dark age (known as *kali-yuga*).

Tantra evolved to help people of the dark age. The revelation of an earlier age was deemed too challenging, and so Tantra developed simpler spiritual practices, notably *mantra* recitation. In actual fact, some of its other methods, especially rituals, are just as demanding as the ancient methods.

Tantra believed that people of the dark age, which supposedly began in 3,002 B.C.E. and will be in effect for many more millennia, would be grasping for straws. Therefore, the Tantric masters allowed any kind of spiritual means, including sexuality. Many schools of Tantra employed methods that mainstream Hindu society considered questionable and even offensive. But the existence of such schools must not blind us to the fact that Tantra has contributed much to Hindu society and culture.

Tantra is a powerful tool, but it has unfortunately been reduced by Westerners to a sexual procedure, which misleadingly goes by the name of "Tantra-Yoga." Georg has dubbed it "Neo-Tantra," as it has little to do with genuine spirituality and a lot with "New Age" thought. Regrettably, some of those who sell Neo-Tantra as a commodity have been quoting Georg's earlier positive comments about authentic Tantra out of context, to give their potential victims the impression that he is favoring their approach; he is *not*. Neither is Brenda.

Years ago, Georg thought that perhaps Neo-Tantra, under skilful guidance, could help those who wanted to sort out their sexual problems. This opinion was entirely too generous and too optimistic. People with sexual problems should see a therapist!

Anyone delving deeper into Hatha-Yoga will inevitably encounter Tantric concepts and practices, some of which we have mentioned earlier. Few people, however, will ever engage Tantra more seriously, because it is incredibly challenging and requires that one adopts many cultural forms and symbols of Hinduism. It remains an esoteric teaching and, unlike Karma-Yoga, requires the guidance and supervision from an initiated teacher.

14. The Teacher: Helper on the Threshold

There are all kinds of teachers. Some pass on useful knowledge or information that allows us to live life more skilfully or competently or that is simply interesting or fascinating. But the traditional teacher of Yoga has a different purpose: His or her goal is to awaken us from our everyday trance, or semi-conscious state, and set us free. Such a teacher is called *guru* (if male) or *gurani* (if female). This Sanskrit term means literally "weighty one." According to an esoteric explanation, the two syllables of the word *guru* suggest "dispeller" (*ru*) of "darkness" (*gu*). Thus, a *guru* is someone who, by virtue of his or her own realization, is qualified to guide us beyond spiritual ignorance, which is ignorance of our true nature and the true nature of the world.

Since realization rarely means "full realization," or "enlightenment," we must not expect every guru to be able to lead us all the way to spiritual liberation. Generally, a guru can take us only as far as he or she has travelled. Yet, he can always point us in the right direction. He *will* do so if he legitimately bears the title *guru.*

Often, a guru is part of a teaching lineage of an entire chain of gurus, and is given permission to teach by his own immediate guru. That's why it is important to have a teacher who belongs to a teaching lineage. Otherwise. anyone can call himself a "guru," which has been a problem in Eastern and Western countries.

Most Yoga centers have Yoga teachers or instructors rather than one or more gurus. The majority of them indeed act only as teachers of physical exercises and have no spiritual pretensions. But you still ought to check out their credentials or reputation. Some teachers acquire certification after a skimpy training of only 200 hours, and sometimes less. Ask around.

Things can become slightly more tricky when meditation is taught. Beginners find it naturally rather difficult to tell the level of accomplishment of a meditation teacher. So, when spiritual advice is given, they have no way of knowing how sound it is. In this case, we must rely on common sense. If something sounds phoney or pretended, it probably is.

Some Yoga teachers also want to teach or advise about spiritual matters, which is fine as long as they don't assume the mantle of a guru. By the way, if you are charged an arm and a leg for meditation instruction or spiritual counsel, we would reconsider. You may well end up with a lot of hogwash.

To learn the Yoga postures, you certainly don't need a guru. If you desire to grow spiritually, you will sooner or later need an authentic Yoga master, or guru. But don't be too quick about finding or settling for a guru. It is better to prepare by taking your Yoga practice as far as you can under your own steam. Work on your emotional and social problems conscientiously, so that when you are in the presence of a genuine guru, you can bring him—or, more rarely, her—the gift of competence.

Traditionally, the disciple was expected to have—in at least undeveloped form—all the virtues, or good qualities, which are associated with mastery in Yoga. Virtues to work on especially are caring, generosity, and patience. These will be expanded through conscious discipline. But your future guru will be grateful for any seeds planted, so that he can water them and help them grow. People with major personality problems cannot really make use of the guru. They will inevitably approach him or her as someone like themselves, which is not the case. Because they see the guru as an "ordinary guy," they will become annoyed or angry with him or her, fighting all the way and not really accepting the help offered. Discipleship should not be the kind of primitive struggle one might have with a parent, a sibling, or a peer.

Psychological resistance is bound to come up in the company of a guru, but the disciple should also be able to deal with it without temper tantrums or even peevishness. Such reactions are entirely unconstructive. The relationship to one's guru is too precious for this kind of childish attitude. Child*like* behavior, on the other hand, is fine. The guru himself might display it when he or she manifests innocent delight or frankness in interaction with others. For the enlightened masters, "others" are not really others.

They *know* that others are the same essence as everyone, and they seek to bring their disciples to the same understanding—the same state of consciousness—as they have.

15. The Disciple: Pilgrim to Reality

When a spiritual seeker stops seeking and starts practicing earnestly, he or she becomes a disciple. Usually this coincides with the appearance of one's guru. Suddenly there is more of a focus or seriousness to one's practice. All of life becomes spiritual discipline. Nor is discipline occasional or haphazard any more, but a sacred obligation. Many of us resent discipline, even the mere word. With the onset of discipleship, however, we have made peace with the basic need for it. We understand that the mind needs to be trained before we can unlock its true potential.

The student is something of a pilgrim, and he or she approaches the pilgrimage of spiritual life as one would any other pilgrimage: with sincerity and gravity. Just as a religious pilgrimage might lead one step by step to a revered shrine, so the yogic pilgrimage leads one, also in a gradual fashion, to the essence of every single being and thing. The disciple understands that this goal might lie far into the future and that the pilgrimage may not be over at the time of death. But he or she is not daunted by this prospect. The important matter is that the disciple is edging closer and closer to the goal. In fact, some Yoga traditions—notably Tantra and radically nondualist Jnana-Yoga—discourage the idea that liberation is a goal. Spiritual freedom is the case here and now, but we really need to realize this.

Indeed, we could awaken in this very moment. The South Indian sage Ramana Maharshi did just that when he was only sixteen years old. Such spontaneous awakenings are rare. Most of us have to buckle down and do the work first. For enlightenment to occur, we need to remove our mental blocks. And this, unfortunately, takes time—many lifetimes in all likelihood.

A disciple does not find prolonged inner work troublesome. He or she knows that no effort is wasted on the path, as the *Bhagavad-Gita* states. Rather, the least struggle to transform ourselves will be in our favor. Sometimes, this may not seem so. In those moments, which may well come, we must remind ourselves that many other disciples have travelled the path and become masters in the end. One's own guru was a disciple once, and no doubt he will also have gone through the struggles of a disciple.

However difficult discipleship becomes, we must not succumb to discouragement, but simply persist. The spiritual path is the way of the hero or heroine who keeps their purpose firmly in mind and does not get ruffled by adversity.

Even a great master cannot relieve a disciple of all bad life experiences, though he or she may well modify the fruit of our karma so as not to interfere with our spiritual efforts. For instance, one's guru might warn about the impending ripening of heavy-duty karma, such as a car accident or the negative consequences of accepting a particular worldly task. But we must learn to listen to the guru with wide-open ears. When adversity is in the offing, then it is up to us to prepare ourselves with as much wisdom as we can muster.

We know that for a psychiatrist or psychotherapist to be able to help a patient, the patient must first establish an emotional connection with him or her (which is known as "transference"). The same is true between a disciple and a guru. Without this link, the alchemy of discipleship cannot work. Is such an emotional link not binding us in some way, you may ask? The answer is a resounding No, because a genuine guru will always ensure that this is not the case. After all, the whole idea is for him or her to help set the disciple free. And the guru would not want to lose his or her own spiritual freedom.

The disciple proceeds on the basis of a powerful ideal, which is to duplicate the guru's spiritual realization or, if possible, surpass it. Therefore, it is vitally important that we work with a guru who embodies our highest ideal or can help us move toward it. If we want to learn quantum physics, we consult someone knowledgeable in this science. We don't rely on the local grocer or music teacher. The guru has first-hand knowledge in the higher realizations of Yoga. He or she is therefore well qualified to show us the path to the same realizations, perhaps even Self-realization.

16. The Path: The Way to Spiritual Freedom

The spiritual process, or work, is frequently portrayed as a path. It is meant to take us beyond our ego-bound state to the ego-free condition of liberation. Freedom from the ego does not necessarily mean having no sense of self, which is really impossible. While we are alive, we inevitably have a body and a mind. When sand or a gnat wants to enter our eyes, we automatically blink. When someone tries to punch us, we duck without thinking about it first. This tells us that there is a sense of self wired into the body itself. But the enlightened being is not egotistical, or ego-bound, as we tend to be. He or she identifies not with the body or mind but with the ultimate reality, the Self.

This state of inner freedom is difficult to imagine. In our unfreedom (which is traditionally called "bondage"), we find it hard to believe that one could function in the world without having this rather solid sense of identity. But we must remember that the ego emerges gradually in us. As far as we know, there is no ego associated with an unborn child, which is simply part of the mother. There is apparently no sense of "I" even in a newborn baby, whose ego is as yet not differentiated from the world. The sense of "I" gradually emerges together with language. Then, during the "terrible twos," the child's ego has crystallized sufficiently to want to assert itself against parental pressure. This development continues on until the child learns to empathize with other people's circumstance or pain.

If this developmental process remains uncompleted, we as adults turn out to be self-centered or even sociopathic. Many people in our contemporary society put their own needs or wants first, what they call "Looking out for Number One." There is no room for an egocentric attitude on the spiritual path. On the contrary, spiritual discipline has the purpose of overcoming all self-cherishing.

Upon enlightenment, the normal sense of identity vanishes, so that the enlightened being regards the body and mind with which he or she was formerly (prior to enlightenment) so closely identified as being no more significant as any other body and mind. If anything, the enlightened master sees his or her "own" body simply as an instrument for serving others. Philosophically, this realization and capacity is rooted in the idea that the ultimate Self is the same Self in everyone.

On the yogic path, then, we unlearn the ways of the ego. We unlearn the habit of wanting to come first, of being a success, or of having it our way. Instead, we are taught to be humble, modest, obliging, respectful, and self-effacing. Eventually, we stop being arrogant, brash, pushy, rough, loud-mouthed, rebellious, unruly, competitive, exaggerated, or purposefully extraordinary. We learn to engage life from a spiritual point of view—simply and without fanfare.

For egocentrics, spiritual life is rather dull and boring. But for true disciples, it is entirely engaging, sane, and whole. They know that the final reward is incomparable, but they do not even egotistically clamor for it. They simply place one foot in front of the other, moved inwardly by the desire for liberation. That desire is far deeper than any egoic desire. It is an impulse that wells up from the depths of the mind until it is fulfilled in Self-realization.

17. Predictable Obstacles

All kinds of possible obstacles exist on the spiritual path. Most of these are self inflicted. Others derive from karma. All are somehow related to the mind, which we must go beyond. In this essay we will consider a few of the most important ones.

Perhaps the most severe obstacle is doubt. We may have doubt about the validity of the spiritual process, the spiritual path, Yoga in particular, or the guru. We may also have self-doubt, that is, doubting our capacity to engage Yoga properly and realize the Self. Such doubt is destructive and a source of suffering.

Studying the wisdom of the masters can remove a certain level of doubt, but if doubt is our form of neurosis, we best seek professional psychological help. Sometimes, a master will assist even with self-doubt, but we must not expect it. The best means of countering doubt is cultivating faith (called *shraddha* in Sanskrit). Faith in oneself and in Yoga is essential. Unlike religious faith, which consists in belief in the creeds or dogmas of one's particular sect or denomination, yogic faith is maintaining a positive attitude. This is called the "mother of Yoga."

Doubt is related to entertaining the "wrong view," a further obstacle. Examples of wrong view would include a gross materialism that denies all the values of Yoga, or the idea that the ego should never be transcended but be carefully kept in place. Wrong view is eliminated by studying the wisdom teachings of Yoga. Some people may find study tedious because they don't understand its value and therefore struggle needlessly with it.

Another common obstacle is heedlessness, or carelessness. In order to succeed on the yogic path we must be constantly mindful. It is so easy to become distracted, and distraction can lead to all kinds of unwelcome entanglements and experiences. For instance, we are resolved to practice Yoga every day, but then there is a TV series that we want to watch, although we know it adds nothing to our life. Still, before we know it, we are watching another alluring program, or even make room for that series in our weekly schedule.

Thus our resolution to practice daily weakens. Many beginning students get distracted in this way. (By the way, Georg and I solved the TV-problem by giving our set away many years ago, and never really missed it.)

Another hurdle to reckon with is apathy. We are apathetic when the mind is too weak to decide on a course of action and stick with it. Other things seem easier to do. To this category of hindrance belongs procrastination: We delay a beneficial activity from one day to another, from one week to another, and so forth.

Closely related is the obstacle of laziness: We are physically too lazy to initiate action. This often happens with people who have a physical imbalance from things such as lack of sleep or a draining diet. Sometimes agreeing to a short and simple physical or study practice is all we need to get started on a different path.

Pleasure seeking, which can be quite addictive, is a formidable enemy on the yogic path. We can become attached to all kinds of pleasant experiences, which seem to be more interesting than Yoga. In a culture that enshrines pleasure and makes it easy on everyone who looks for pleasurable experiences, we find it particularly hard to do anything that does not offer immediate gratification. Self-realization, or enlightenment, is likely to be a long-term affair. Although according to various traditions there are some individuals who have made swift progress toward the achievement of enlightenment, this is the exception, and we would be foolish to expect it. Our focus should be on yogic practice, regardless of how long it will take to go beyond the ego and realize the Self. In due course, treading the spiritual path becomes a daily joy. Or at least, we no longer struggle against it by struggling with ourselves.

Depression, which is epidemic in our modern society, is considered a major obstacle on the path. Often this is a physical problem, such as a food allergy or lack of sunshine. But it can also have psychological causes, which we ought to unravel through psychotherapy or in some other way. The other way is Yoga. While depression can—but need not—slow down the spiritual process, a regular posture and breathing practice can work wonders. Yoga teacher Amy Weintraub has written an excellent book entitled *Yoga for Depression*: A *Compassionate Guide To Relieve Suffering*

Through Yoga. (New York: Broadway Books, 2004), which we can heartily recommend.

If we go deeper into the spiritual aspect of Yoga, we find that some forms of depression are caused simply by our inability to take the Self into account. We must learn to see our depressive tendencies in a new light. They are just mind. We are not our feelings of depression. We can, as Weintraub explained, witness our feelings and thus stand apart. This standing apart is in fact crucial in Yoga. It is the foundation of discernment without which Self-realization is unlikely to occur.

18. Self-Discipline: Necessary Restraint

The spiritual path involves self-discipline to a high degree. The ordinary person is generally averse to self-discipline and prefers a self-cherishing attitude instead. Obviously we take great pleasure in our opinions and words, or why would we engage in idle talk quite so frivolously? We could be said to revere ourselves, and we certainly prefer that others think highly of us. Some people notoriously insist on being the center of attention. They are equipped with an inflated ego that wants to, and often does, deflate everyone else. The bigger the ego, it seems, the more one likes to trumpet their merits, even when everyone has heard about them already, or is not at all interested.

But, regardless of the size of our ego, we all "throw off" energy recklessly. Our senses are constantly searching for distractions that can lead us to consuming far too much. A lot of energy is wasted this way, and our attention is constantly bound up in matters that can hardly be said to be either life-sustaining or imperative.

Self-discipline, as the word suggests, is exercising conscious control over our ego, or "little" self and the two instruments—body and mind—by which we express ourselves. Normally, we like to live as we want. This desire is restrained only by the pressure of other people's expectations, as they have their own personal preferences that may interfere with ours.

Children on a playground may cooperate amazingly, but their play may also sometimes devolve into bedlam, with each one pretty much wanting to realize his or her own desires. This self-centeredness does not work in any society, and any hint of such anarchy will be resisted by the mainstream. The idea behind this resistance is for life to flow along as smoothly and peacefully as possible. No one wants his feathers ruffled, and authorities like to be in control, which is possible only when everyone conforms.

The situation is different in Yoga. Here a practitioner is not expected to merely "conform" but to "*trans*form," that is, to consciously adopt attitudes and behaviors that are constructive on the spiritual path. True enough, there have been many "misfits" in Hindu Yoga—*yogis* who do not play by the rules, who go about naked, wear their hair in dreadlocks, are jobless, have no income, and flout any sort of polite or decent behavior. For their own reasons, they purposefully defy polite social conduct. Yet, with themselves, they may be rather strict and austere.

The main purpose of self-discipline is to train the mind, that is, to make it pliable for the higher work in meditation, and for sound living. An undisciplined mind, as we may know only too well from our own experience, is not able to meditate and is easily shaken up by life's harsher experiences. So, the Yoga practitioner is charged with bringing the mind under control, especially the many desires that pull it hither and thither.

Before we can attempt to discipline the mind, however, we must first understand that it needs disciplining. This is far from obvious to some people. They do not look deeply enough and hence don't see the storm of their desires, the ups and downs of their emotions, or the fickleness of their mind. They wrongly assume that "all's perfect" with them, so there is no need for improvement.

The sincere Yoga practitioner, however, knows that there is plenty of room for developing his or her inner potential by transforming both the mind and the personality. The good qualities a guru would be looking for in a disciple need to be deliberately cultivated. These qualities don't grow on their own like grass or thistles. A garden calls for regular and mindful care or it will not flourish. Similarly, the mind will turn to the equivalent of weeds when it is not cared for properly. If the weed metaphor does not sit well with you, then think of the uncultivated mind as a junkyard stripped of all re-useable materials.

Self-discipline requires that we consciously take the initiative and then persist, regardless of the "temptations" that life conjures up for us. These range from passively watching television hour after hour while unconsciously consuming junk food, to becoming high on drugs, or drunk on alcohol, entering into casual sexual relationships, and seeking out the company of people who have no interest in spiritual life but indulge at will in their materialist desires.

Yoga masters do not indulge their desires but stand ready to help whoever needs help, or to teach when their pupils are ready to really listen to the yogic teachings. There is no ounce of selfishness in a bona fide master. He or she really lives for the benefit of others. The genuine guru has no personal preferences, although he or she may come across otherwise when pressed to choose. The guru's true preference is to communicate his or her own realization to disciples, so that they too can one day be completely free in themselves. The guru's desireless disposition is due to having realized an extraordinary state of equanimity. Because of this, he or she radiates a tangible peace that in itself can prove transformative for disciples.

19. Community: Strength in Numbers

The life of a disciple in the midst of conventional society is not easy. Especially in our own time, the distractions are numerous and persistent. Solitude, which was recommended in the past as a major transformative tool, is hardly any longer available. Nor is our social environment of average people with conventional interests necessarily supportive. When television, football, bar hopping and other similar pursuits lose their hold on a Yoga practitioner, he or she increasingly feels the need for a support system. This comes in the form of a community of like-minded and like-hearted practitioners (called *sangha* in Sanskrit). This is not the usual coffee-and-gossip clique. Instead, the *sangha* is a group of fellow disciples who are interested in practicing together or in talking about the teachings. Some, hopefully benign, gossip is natural. But the common focus is very much on the spiritual process of self-transformation.

Not every *sangha*, of course, meets this ideal. If the shoe doesn't fit, as they say, try elsewhere. Or, if there is any openness at all, you might endeavor to introduce a different attitude as long as you do it humbly and skillfully. If you encounter resistance, kindly and politely move on. You are certainly not the only person practicing with serious intention. You may not find a fellow pilgrim on the path in your local area but you surely will in another district or a nearby town.

You may feel tempted to practice by yourself. There is no problem if you can do this without feeling superior to others or simply resentful. Even then, however, you would certainly benefit from at least occasional participation in a group of dedicated practitioners. There is definitely strength in numbers. Besides, if you have a guru and want to spend time in his or her company, you are bound to find him or her surrounded by disciples. The guru might only sit quietly or deliver an inspiring talk. At any rate, his or her presence is predictably exhilarating but also inherently demanding, because the guru's mere presence represents a challenge from within the disciple's mind. The challenge is a steady call for transformation, for waking up as the Self.

Even gurus who have not yet become enlightened can be rather demanding in this way. They call their disciples from deep within or urge them on verbally. Often they are more demanding than enlightened masters, who know that enlightenment is a game that the mind plays. The Self is always the same free being, and therefore there is absolutely no urgency. The only urgency that exists is to help those for whom suffering is still a very real experience and who, if they are spiritual pupils, struggle to realize enlightenment.

Some *yogins* pursued liberation far removed from ordinary people in the isolation of a cave, a jungle, or a remote hut. Others did their best to attain enlightenment or a lower spiritual realization in the company of others. These traditional texts and teachers normally exhorted people to seek out the company of realized masters or at least (in the yogic sense) virtuous people. The *sangha*, then, is a group of virtuous Yoga practitioners, who pursue the spiritual goal of freedom with integrity.

Aspiring Yoga practitioners are not without desires, but they seek to cultivate only those desires that do not thwart the spiritual process. As they move along on the path, their desires become ever fewer and ever more simple. They should not, of course, repress desires unless they are truly destructive. They learn to enjoy inner stillness more than boisterous external activity.

20. Ego-Transcendence: Beyond I, Me, and Mine

Transcending, or going beyond, the ego is a central undertaking in spiritual work. Yogic self-transformation basically consists in this: We are asked to, bit by bit, retire the egotism we acquired in the course of a lifetime and instead nurture an attitude of wholesome altruism. The qualifying word "wholesome" is necessary, because there is also toxic altruism. Such altruism is toxic because it is self-centered. It leads to self-poisoning. Wholesome altruism, by contrast, is free from self-centeredness and is truly in the service of others without proving damaging to oneself.

Research has proven that humans are not natural predators, nor are they by instinct aggressive rather than cooperative. We actually are by nature more inclined to cooperate with others. In Yoga, self-transcendence is a central virtue. The yogic process cannot succeed without it. Enlightenment, the goal of Yoga, is consummate self-transcendence.

How can we transcend the ego when the ego is constantly in our face until the moment we become enlightened? This question is not correctly formulated, because we are enlightened even now. We have always been enlightened and will be so into the most distant future. The Self, who we truly are, is always enlightened. At one point, we merely recognize this inescapable fact. It is true that we tend to identify not with the Self but the body and mind—thus creating the ego. But by recognizing the Self and inching closer to it, we can out-maneuver the ego. The ego cannot enlighten us. By gradually diminishing it, however, we can be our true Self, our innermost essence.

Every kind act is a form of self-transcendence. Every time we give a gift for unselfish reasons, we practice self-transcendence. Every exercise in patience is a form of self-transcendence. Every compassionate gesture is self-transcendence in action. Thus we can move, slowly but surely, toward Self-realization, or enlightenment:

We act enlightened. We think enlightened. We feel enlightened. We speak enlightened. It is this simple.

Some people feel that we must meditate in order to attain Self-realization. This is not so. Meditation is helpful in quieting the mind. But, as Jnana-Yoga teaches us, meditation adds nothing to our innate enlightenment. If it is done selfishly, it foils our recognition of enlightenment to boot. As the *Bhagavad-Gita* (12.12) tells us, meditation is higher than knowledge, but abandoning self-centered activity is higher than meditation.

There is, then, nothing mysterious about Yoga and the way to the Self. Of course, going beyond the grip of the ego is challenging. It is our normal state of existence. We even endorse and celebrate the ego when we are encouraged to build it up, strengthen, toughen, or improve it by the competitive business environment. Our civilization doesn't seem to care for the Self. By and large, it doesn't even know about its existence. We tend to honour the person who is a "successful" ego instead of seeing that as a hindrance.

From a spiritual perspective, however, the ego is little more than a cause and manifestation of suffering. This is perhaps difficult to grasp. The difficulty disappears when we think of the ego as a masquerade—a false sense of identity by which we maintain the functions of unenlightened life. The Self is our rightful or real identity. When we take all our masks off, by practicing self-transcendence, we will inevitably become who we always are.

The charade we play is entertaining only as long as we and our fellow players are engaged in the same pretence. As soon as we tire of playing the game that seems to hold everyone spellbound, we have no choice but to play the far more interesting game of self-transcendence. This game has a different set of rules, which we discover as we go along. It certainly is far more benign than the ordinary game played by virtually all those who have no inkling about the Self and take their conventional concerns with extreme seriousness. That is, they behave as if even their genuinely serious concerns are of any consequence in the larger scheme of things. From the Self's point of view, all is a charade, a make-believe game. We have dressed up and taken our self-adopted roles with humourless seriousness.

We don't realize that when we take our costume and mask off, we are free.

21. Wisdom

Wisdom is not prominent in our time, which more values knowledge and information. Only very recently, perhaps because we are beginning to recognize the shortcomings of knowledge, has wisdom become an object of scientific (psychological) curiosity and investigation. Yoga, however, is packed with wisdom. The yogic masters may be somewhat ignorant in conventional terms, but they are full of wisdom. Therefore, we can confidently turn to them for wise help on the spiritual path.

The teachings of the great Yoga masters are available to us in book form in the *Bhagavad-Gītā* and the *Yoga-Sūtra of Patañjali*. Since wisdom is ageless, it is as relevant today as it was a thousand or more years ago. But we must be open to finding and applying that significance in our own situations. The outer circumstances have undoubtedly changed in the course of time. The mind, however, has remained quite constant, and the problems of an earlier age are often the same as today.

In the state of ecstasy, which comes at the peak of the spiritual path prior to final liberation, or enlightenment, the practitioner knows everything as one. We realize that all things are interconnected. For our era, which is experiencing the first "inconvenient" consequences of a flawed attitude toward Nature, this recognition that "all is one" is important wisdom. While surprisingly large numbers of people experience ecstatic or ecstasy-like moments, presumably few of us will realize yogic ecstasy in a consciously generated manner. But we can heed the wisdom of the masters, which tells us that there are states of consciousness in which we can and do experience the unity of Nature firsthand.

Their wisdom tells us, among other things, that in order to live peacefully and healthily, we must live in harmony with Nature. This is not what we have done in the past 200 years. We are now learning in a painful way that we were mistaken in thinking that Earth's resources were inexhaustible. The few highly-industrialized countries have ransacked the world to build "civilization" to an artificial height. Our brothers and sisters in the larger underdeveloped parts of the world are paying for our inconsiderateness and greed in many ways. Wisdom tells us that this is unjust, unscrupulous, and unwise.

The spiritual path has been called a "razor's edge." A great deal of wisdom is required to tread it. Yoga gives us such wisdom. In particular, it shows us how to distinguish between the real and the unreal. At the ultimate end of the path is Self-realization, or actual enlightenment. For the sages of Yoga, unreal is everything that is not the Self, not pure awareness. This includes the mind. Even when it is steeped in wisdom, they regard the mind as falling short of the reality of the Self, which is our essential nature.

The masters of Yoga understood that the mind exists, like the Moon, on borrowed light. The Moon does not give off heat or warmth but only reflected light, which comes from the Sun. If the Self is similar to the Sun, it makes sense to want to realize it. By itself, the mind cannot sustain us. But, so the sages tell us, the Self can, since it is our true identity. We only mistakenly identify with the mind. Many people even think that they *are* the brain-mind.

Training in Yoga shows that identification with "brain-mind" alone is not the real story. It has been demonstrated scientifically that there are states of mind that clearly go beyond the brain. "Near-death experiences" are one example. They indicate that the brain can be totally disabled while mental states happily continue.

Self-realization happens *without* the mind. Certainly awareness is ever present, yet the mind can come and go. This does not imply unconsciousness, however. The sages would not have aspired to this, as their goal has always been to realize the Self, which is the identity of every living being and even of the insentient natural world.

The masters of Yoga discipline the mind in order to be able to consciously go beyond it. It is difficult to fathom their consummate skill in controlling the mind. When we sit down to meditate, the mind chatters on by itself. We cannot even imagine that the mind could stop for more than a few seconds at a time. Yet, this has been the experience of every Yoga practitioner who persists. The mind can become as docile as a puppy.

Wisdom stands at both the beginning threshold and as the lofty goal of Yoga. At first, wisdom guides us to inner freedom. In the end, upon living liberation (that is, Self-realization while still embodied), the Self mysteriously inspires the mind to spawn wisdom for the benefit of others.

Wisdom is the quality of a highly refined mind, which is replete with lucidity. For this to be the case, the mind has to be similar to the Self. That is to say, it must be as still and as luminous as possible. Even if the mind cannot produce its own light, it can reflect it. This reflected luminosity is wisdom.

22. Proper Livelihood: Integrity in All Matters

To put it bluntly: If you aspire to be a bank director, you cannot also be a bank robber. Similarly, if you aspire toward mastery in Yoga, you cannot also be a moral good-for-nothing. It is important for a Yoga practitioner to pursue a proper livelihood. That means earning one's living in a decent and respectable way that does not violate any of Yoga's many moral virtues. Another way of putting this is to say that we should cultivate integrity in all matters, including the work we do.

Would it be appropriate for a Yoga practitioner to be a hired overseas enforcer for an international corporation, a factory farmer, a casino manager, or a lobbyist for a cut-throat pharmaceutical company? We think not. All these jobs involve unsavoury practices or goals that definitely compromise a Yoga practitioner's moral integrity. We actually had a student who, attracted by a handsome salary, took on a job at a casino. Before very long, he found that the atmosphere in the casino was so disagreeable that at the end of the day he felt filthy and didn't even want to continue with his practice of Yoga. In the end, he resigned and has never regretted his decision.

We cannot practice integrity part-time, or in one corner of our life but not in all respects. Integrity cannot be compartmentalized; it is an all-or-nothing matter. We regard integrity as an aspect of truthfulness, which is considered a major virtue in Patanjali's Yoga and, of course, in other branches of Yoga as well. He tells us that when a practitioner is firmly established in truthfulness, whatever he or she affirms comes true. We personally would limit this ability to spiritual matters, because in worldly affairs a master often relies, like everyone else, primarily on information that may or may not be entirely correct. As a rule, however, a master does not indulge in chitchat or unconsidered opinions.

Regretfully, the contemporary Yoga movement in the West lacks integrity in several respects. The first is that many Yoga teachers give the wrong impression that Yoga is no more than postural practice. This is unfair to traditional Yoga, which is obviously very much more. It is also unfair to newcomers to Yoga who don't know any better but should be given an opportunity to explore the spirituality of Yoga and the full range of its practices.

Most deplorable is the absence of traditional Yoga's moral disciplines from many of the teachings offered at modern centers. This is like offering a person a chair with only three legs to sit on, which is an accident in the making. What good, one may ask, will it do for a student to know the headstand if, when he or she has a car accident, they do not know how to manage life afterward? Or, of what advantage is mastering the Warrior III pose when the mind is worrying about death?

Not only is modern Yoga by and large not grounded in the moral precepts, it is also shot through with the moral apathy and shallowness that mark our mainstream culture. It is irresponsible for a Yoga teacher to tell his or her students, as we have heard, that the moral disciplines are unimportant. In fact, without them there can be no attainment of mental health, never mind inner freedom. And it is negligent for a Yoga teacher to publicly debunk the spiritual orientation of Yoga, because this is precisely what is missing from our troubled culture. Integrity, among other things, means to present and practice Yoga as the spiritual tradition that it is. Anything less is dishonest.

23. Diet: You Are What You Eat

People certainly don't think of themselves as turkeys after eating their standard Thanksgiving dinner, or as chickens when they have consumed "white meat," or as "pigs" after eating the "red meat" known as pork.

The fact is, though, that our food substantially affects us not only physiologically but also mentally. Some people find this hard to believe. Even the best food is made up of chemicals, and when these chemicals enter our bloodstream, they inevitably impact on body and mind. Think of ice cream, potato dumplings, or the Sunday roast, which in larger amounts all make us feel physically stuffed, heavy and mentally sluggish. A light salad meal, by contrast, is likely to make us feel physically light, and possibly mentally lightheaded. Mothers know that when children consume a lot of sugar, they become giddy and unfocused.

On the yogic path, much attention is paid to the food we eat. *Yogins* want their body and mind to function optimally. What, then, is an optimal diet? This question has been answered in widely-read books like John Robbins' *Diet for a New America* and Dr. Gabriel Cousens' *Conscious Eating*. Taking into account recent research, they concluded that people will thrive on a balanced vegetarian diet consisting of vegetables, nuts, seeds, and adequate amounts of vegetable oil. They support very few dairy products, but no meat or fish.

As Karl Weber's edited volume *Food, Inc.* has documented, "industrial" or "fast" food—that is, the typical supermarket food—is making everyone sicker. The reason for this is that it has little nutritional value and also contains dangerous chemicals (such as food coloring, preservatives, growth hormones, and antibiotics). Today, the food supply is in the hands of surprisingly few large corporations, which exist to make as much profit as possible. They are not concerned about people's health. Nor are they concerned about the devastating effect which industrial agriculture has on the environment. The food industry is a major polluter of soil, water, and air. (We have written about this in our book *Green Yoga.*)

In the U.S.A., the Department of Agriculture and the Food and Drug Administration, who are supposed to exist for the benefit of the consumer, condone and endorse this industrial scam, which is outrageous and disheartening. The U.S. government also grants substantial subsidies to these corporations to keep them going, which is a self-defeating practice, because we are getting sicker and sicker and health costs are rising.

For Yoga practitioners wanting to observe the cardinal virtue of nonharming, there is the additional issue over the abusive treatment of "factory" animals. For example, a factory farm might squeeze hundreds of thousands of chickens and other poultry into a comparatively small area and never allow them to see the light of day. Because of the crowded conditions, the chickens peck each other rather than morsels on the ground, and consequently factory farmers clip their beaks. The birds are given antibiotics for faster growth, and some birds grow so heavy that their legs buckle. Painful bone deformities are common. The slaughter house experience is just as traumatic and unconscionable.

This is just a small glimpse into the meat industry. We felt compelled to say something about this, because all too many people—including Yoga practitioners—are still ignorant of these unsavory facts. It is easy to see how our chosen diet has far-reaching consequences, which are indeed inconvenient but should not be ignored if we wish to live ethically and healthily.

24. Liberation: Spiritual Freedom Now or Later

Spiritual liberation is realization of our innermost essence, the Self. This can occur after death or even before the body and mind have disintegrated. The latter form of freedom is known as "living liberation." It is qualitatively the same as the former and is often known as enlightenment.

In both cases, the mind must be fully transcended. That is to say, there must be nothing in the way of pure awareness. While we are alive, Self-realization is a paradoxical state. On one hand, there is the disembodied, eternal Self, and on the other hand, there is the finite body and an equally finite mind. This is a mind-boggling combination!

The Self-realized adept who is alive has pushed the mind to its limits, such that it barely exists at all. Certainly, the adept's mind includes no tendency toward self-centeredness. In some cases, the master may spend more time being present as the Self. In (most) other cases, he or she dips into actual Self-realization periodically, which then has a profoundly transformative effect on the mind. Put differently, in the Self-realized adept, the Self—or God—is more present than the mind.

The process of Yoga is an unveiling of the ever-present Self. We are always free, or liberated. But the blocks in our mind prevent us from recognizing our innate freedom. This is comparable to a tree branch standing in the way of the Sun. When we bend the branch a little, the sunlight strikes our eyes. When we remove the obstructions in the mind—all the negative emotions like anger, lust, greed, and so on—we can welcome the light of the Self in our heart. Even a little bit of the yogic work can give us a glimpse of the Self. In a way, every step toward the Self is liberating.

Yoga is thus excavation work, which gets rid of the dross in the psyche. At first, this requires a very muscular effort. We have to apply ourselves systematically using willpower and self-discipline. Imagine spade and pickaxe. Later on, the yogic work becomes more subtle but also more challenging, because the impediments are not always easy to see. When you are still in the process of dismantling gross self-centeredness, you will in general know what to do. More subtle forms of self-centeredness involve mental obstacles that call for great discernment. It may not always be obvious to a disciple even which functions of the mind are self-centered. This is where a guru can be supremely helpful. He or she has struggled with the same or a similar problem.

Being more skilful on the ecstatic circuit of the spiritual path, the guru can point out where we are getting sidetracked. The experience of ecstasy—either in its lower forms or by dint of artificial means (such as drugs or *mantras*)—can itself be full of traps. Not every ecstasy reveals the Self. The ecstatic state can, however, look like the real thing. Only superior discernment—like a teacher is apt to have—will settle the matter.

Whenever we are close to Self-realization, our conduct is likely to become simple and inspiring to others. The nondual Self, after all, is simple. As long as our life is overly convoluted, or complicated, we are still closer to the mind than to the Self. On the spiritual path, the mind is progressively stripped of the need for complication and extraordinariness. In fact, disciples are to all appearances ordinary people. They don't wear a special sign that proclaims: "I am a disciple." Nor do disciples engage in extraordinary feats. If they do, then we ought to question their spiritual status. To *behave* in an ordinary manner while *being* extraordinary on the inside is a sign of freedom.

The freer we are, the less likely do we feel the urge to assert ourselves or display our specific neuroses. The liberated being is non-neurotic. He or she has overcome the wiles and compulsions of the mind.

PART TWO

Questions and Answers

Prelude

The following questions are selected from among many we have responded to over the years. We trust that our answers might be helpful to you and others. At the same time, we believe that, with a little reflection, most questions can be answered by the questioners themselves, relying on their own common sense and innate wisdom.

Questions and Answers

1. I am a Christian. Can I practice Yoga without jeopardizing my faith?

With the growing popularity of Yoga, this has become a widespread issue. Quite a few people agonize over this. We realize this is an important matter, and so we want to give a carefully differentiated answer. Let's start by saying: It all depends on what yogic method or approach you wish to engage.

As Part One of this book makes clear, Yoga is not a religion, though some branches of Yoga—notably Bhakti-Yoga—have a strong religious coloring. So, despite the common ground of devotion/love, it would presumably not work for a Christian to practice Hindu Bhakti-Yoga. There is, however, no ideological reason preventing anyone from practicing a good many of the methods of Hatha-Yoga, such as postures, breath control, relaxation, diet, and so on.

Moreover, the moral disciplines of Yoga have much in common with Christian ethics, but anyone with a strong commitment to Christianity can be expected to practice these disciplines already. This aspect of Yoga is incredibly important. Actually, we would argue that the moral disciplines are the most important limb of Yoga, especially for contemporary people. Unfortunately, this limb is frequently ignored and even belittled. There is also absolutely no harm in practicing Karma-Yoga whose working principles match the ethics of Christianity.

Practicing Raja-Yoga, Jnana-Yoga, or Tantra-Yoga, or adopting a yogic meditation practice may be a different kettle of fish. Personally, we would recommend that a Christian stick with a Christian form of meditation rather than feel compromised by a Hindu type of meditation. Many people are not even aware that Christianity has evolved its own systems of meditation, such as the routines developed by St. Ignatius of Loyola in the sixteenth century, or the Heart Prayer of the Eastern Orthodox Church, and others. The closer your religious practice is to Christian mysticism—aspects of which are misunderstood or challenged by individuals or various groups within Christianity—the less likely you will be disturbed by the spirituality of Yoga.

Most Yoga centers in the West focus on the postures and, to our dismay, do not teach the other aspects of Yoga. So, Christians may not be exposed at all to the spiritual side of Yoga. However, if a Yoga teacher has a more traditional and inclusive approach, anyone is free to abstain from participating in methods or considerations that rub the wrong way, or to refrain from returning to that center or class. Some religious authorities do worry and even assert that simply by practicing the postures, a person is risking their faith by involving themselves in the forms of another religious system. Ultimately, each practitioner must make an informed decision for him- or herself.

2. I am strongly drawn to Hinduism. How can I get more involved?

Hinduism is first and foremost a culture. It has so many aspects, and the best way of proceeding is to study and then study some more. We can *immerse* ourselves into a culture but cannot *convert* to it. There are many teachers who treat Hinduism as a religion and offer to initiate applicants. This usually involves a sort of conversion to a specific Hindu tradition, such as Shaivism (revolving around Shiva) or Vaishnavism (revolving around Vishnu). It is best to proceed slowly. One way of finding "your" niche is by becoming associated with a local Hindu community or, if you have to, by spending time in India.

3. Where can I find a guru?

This is a question that is asked often and prematurely. But a better question is: *How* can I find a guru? One doesn't need a guru to perform the postures or relaxation techniques. A good Yoga instructor will do. A guru is, however, necessary for growth in the more advanced stages of yogic practice. Most people worry too early about finding a guru. In the past, we would typically share with them a piece of traditional wisdom: The guru will find you! This message would either make them disappointed or angry with us. Nevertheless, we will repeat the same message here.

It makes no sense for a toddler to ask for instruction from a university professor. Toddlers have to learn many other lessons first. The average seeker is much like a toddler—eager to explore but unprepared, with few skills.

The best way of finding one's guru is to steadfastly prepare for this eventuality by practicing the limbs of Yoga as wholeheartedly as possible. An unprepared person would not even recognize his or her guru. There is no better gift we could offer our guru than to approach with an understanding of the rudiments of the spiritual process, and with a flexible and eager personality with which the guru can work. That means we have to learn gratitude, respect, and the willingness to change.

4. Why do you write Yoga with a capital Y?

A good question. Few people write the name of a spiritual tradition—like Christianity, Judaism, Vedanta, Samkhya, Zen, or Buddhism with a lower-case initial. This looks strange to our eye. It seems to put such traditions on a par with gymnastics or acrobatics. Yoga is a fully fledged spiritual tradition and, we think, deserves an initial capital. Some people have suggested that when you write *yoga*, with a lower-case initial, you refer only to postural practice. This attitude accepts the status quo, which on a certain level we don't. We would much rather see postural practice flower into Yoga proper, and in that case an upper-case initial is definitely in order.

5. My partner has no interest in Yoga, but my own interest is deepening. This has become a problem. What should I do?

This same question was put to Georg when he was teaching yogic postures in his early twenties, having little experience with married life, and having almost as little wisdom. Wanting to be helpful, he fumbled his way through some sort of a meaningful response. Many years later he would answer: Develop your own interest, but don't expect your partner to follow. Instead, practice great tolerance and a positive attitude toward your partner. Also, find as much common ground as possible, ideally before making a marital commitment.

6. I have a very busy life. How can I accommodate Yoga properly?

This is a common question and complaint. In our Western culture, everyone is busy. We feel we have to earn as much as possible, not realizing that we pay more in taxes, suffer from ill health due to stress, have large mortgage payments, and on and on.

The real question is not how to *squeeze* Yoga into our busy schedules, but how to prioritize our values, goals, commitments, etc. Many people have concluded, wisely, that they are much too busy, and have started to simplify their life. Some have relocated; others have opted for a less demanding and less well-paying job, or have decided to reduce their consumerism. This takes guts, but, as many families have demonstrated, it can be done.

7. I like meat. Can I still practice nonharming?

If you consume meat, your practice of nonharming is inevitably compromised. You will harm indirectly by supporting the meat industry, which is known to be brutal toward animals. As long as we are alive, we cannot avoid doing harm. But we can minimize this effect, for instance, by choosing a diet that is as benign as possible. Just because we like something does not give us the right to do harm or to endorse harmful practices.

There is now sufficient scientific evidence to show that a vegetarian diet is optimal. Entire cultures have lived on such a diet for centuries, and their populations are as healthy as any other.

We invite anyone preferring a meat diet to watch one of the PETA documentaries or the documentary *Earthlings*.

Apart from health reasons, abstaining from meat eating is a crucial ethical matter.

8. When I read Yoga classics, I find them rather mythological, religious, and illogical. This prevents me from starting a Yoga practice.

Is there a bias at work here? Humans do tend to see what they expect to see.

Based in our own research, study and practice over many years, we can assure you that by no means are all Yoga texts either mythological or religious. Certainly we do encounter symbolism, spirituality, and formidable logical arguments, and we also are called to face some rather inconvenient truths that these texts put forth.

Generally, we don't start a Yoga practice because we don't want to be challenged by it.

This is just a thought we offer for your consideration.

9. I try to practice Yoga every day. Sometimes I just don't have the time, which makes me feel very guilty. What should I do?

We have answered this question in part by what we said in answer #5.

As far as guilt is concerned, it is appropriate to feel this emotion when we have done wrong. Otherwise, guilt is neurotic and an entirely unconstructive emotion that merely hinders us.

Instead of indulging in guilt, we would recommend making the most of *whatever* practice (with whatever frequency) one has been able to establish. It is better to rejoice in Yoga than to focus on the negative circumstances preventing us from engaging it as often or as intensively as we would like.

10. I want to meditate, but my mind is racing all the time. What can I do about this?

Over 2,000 years ago, Prince Arjuna asked this same question of the enlightened master Krishna in the *Bhagavad-Gita*. Krishna assured him that the mind can in fact be controlled. In our own times, while it is quite likely that the mind *is* racing faster than in previous millennia, still, in principle, the truth abides—the mind can be controlled! We may, however, have to enlist some extra help to calm the mind, such as uncluttering and simplifying our lifestyle, by delegating or not taking on quite so many tasks and obligations.

It is in the nature of the mind to produce thoughts. Even a little bit of conscious relaxation or meditation can thin out our thoughts and create mental space. In the early stages of meditation practice, it is natural for thoughts to boil on and on, leaving us with the impression that we will never gain mastery over our mind. Wrong impression! As we sit in meditation regularly (daily), we find that the mind slows down, and maybe even slows down considerably sooner than we assumed.

As neurologists have discovered in recent years, the brain is surprisingly adaptable. Contrary to previous opinion, brain cells can in fact regenerate throughout our lifespan. Regular meditation will retrain the brain, so that gradually meditation will become easier and "successful." The mind will stop racing and begin to settle down. Later, it will go beyond its assumed boundaries, and still later it will find itself in the sublime state of ecstasy.

11. I think that Yoga is self-hypnosis. What's your response?

In the 1930s, researchers thought that Yoga was based on self-hypnosis. This view is generally not supported today, however. While certain relaxation and meditation practices do involve aspects of this hypnotic mechanism (to the advantage of the *yogin*), such an overall categorization cannot be applied to all of Yoga. The science of Yoga is traditionally well aware of the state of hypnosis, but for the most part does not employ it in its spiritual repertoire.

Even if Yoga were mostly self-hypnosis, which it is not, what would be wrong with it if this could produce positive results in one's personal health or social interactions? If anything, Yoga enables its practitioners to engage the "real" world with eyes open, not in some state of trance, and with a healthily realistic attitude.

12. I have been practicing Yoga on and off for many years. My problem is I easily fall off the wagon. Is there a remedy for this?

Why do people suddenly drop their spiritual discipline only to resume it later on, probably with lots of guilt feelings? This usually happens when practice becomes difficult or when a worldly matter (a job, a love affair, etc.) becomes overwhelmingly attractive. That's why Yoga emphasizes the need to be attentive from moment to moment. When we ski down a steep slope, we may move too fast to look behind us, or may look up into the sky to admire a bird. In order to avoid sudden obstacles, however, it is wise to concentrate on the path opening up before us.

The spiritual path is similarly fast, and it abounds with potential hurdles. Therefore, we ought to cultivate mindfulness in every moment. Life always throws us curve balls; we must learn how to meet them properly, so that we don't get thrown off balance and lose our way.

13. There are many things I don't like about my guru, and I have been struggling with this for some time. I fear that leaving him would be very upsetting for him. What should I do?

We can only offer general advice, because each situation is unique. On the spiritual path, liking or not liking one's guru is irrelevant. It is, of course, helpful and probably even necessary to have a basically positive attitude toward one's guru.

The guru's job is to promote the spiritual process in the disciple. This is never a pleasant undertaking, because the guru has to undermine all the things that stand in the way of the disciple's realization of freedom. Most of these things have to do with the disciple's personality, wrong assumptions, false expectations, and other unpalatable issues. So, the guru is inevitably "in the disciple's face"—a most ungrateful task.

Predictably, disciples resent this sort of interference. Some confuse the guru with an ordinary teacher, who is concerned with passing on information. Ordinary teachers do not assume responsibility for their disciples' spiritual welfare. The guru's area of competence is mental and spiritual transformation. They have the right and tacit permission to intervene in a disciple's personal life.

In this connection it is also worth considering: Contrary to popular belief, most gurus are *not* enlightened. They still have to deal with their own ego. But even an enlightened guru has a personality. If we don't resonate with the guru's personality, it is best not to become his or her disciple. Once we have taken this step, however, it is best to roll with the punches unless one's guru's personality really stands in the way of our own inner growth. This should be assessed carefully, primarily through introspection and perhaps in consultation with others. We should never leave a guru just because we don't like certain things about him or her.

That's why it is okay to do some "guru shopping" before making a real commitment. The guru will similarly examine the prospective pupil. But once the guru-disciple relationship has seriously started—often by initiation—one's guru should not be casually abandoned. There are, however, serious reasons for leaving one's guru, especially in the case of obvious sexual abuse or because one has stopped growing spiritually over a period of time. Even then, we really ought to examine the matter carefully.

A fully enlightened guru simply does not engage in egoically-motivated actions. As we said, such guru*s* are exceedingly rare, perhaps one in 500 million (just a guess!). Many of the guru*s* that claim enlightenment for themselves or have others do it on their behalf are questionable. By traditional standards, some are clearly not enlightened. Brenda has a good rule: Look for those qualities in your guru which you would eventually like to realize yourself.

When we have had the extreme good fortune of having come into contact with an enlightened master, we should endeavour to make a lifelong commitment to discipleship and stick with it even when the going gets rough, and it will.

Finally, if one's guru gets upset or angry about you leaving, that is really his or her business. It means that he or she still has to go beyond the ego. The only feeling that would arise in an enlightened master is regret for the disciple. But such regret would be mixed with a bundle of genuinely good wishes for the "lost" pupil.

14. I am an atheist. Can I still practice Yoga?

Atheism is an ideology, and some atheists cling to it with as much fervor as others cling to their religion. Yet, no unenlightened person can tell for sure whether there is a God, or not. Therefore, we find agnosticism both more plausible logically and also a more humble attitude: We simply don't know. To affirm that there is no God implies all sorts of assumptions, which are usually based on materialistic science. But that kind of science has itself come under challenge of late. More and more philosophers and even scientists themselves are calling for a new paradigm, a new non-materialistic worldview, which can explain things—meaning the findings of science—more satisfactorily. Be that as it may, much of what we said in answer #1 applies also to an atheist, minus our recommendations for a Christian.

15. Do I really need a guru to attain Self-realization?

Yes, unless a person is a spiritual genius, but this very question implies otherwise. Most spiritual seekers, who are fewer than 99.99 percent of us, need significant help in order to realize the ultimate essence. But, as we explain in this book, to be able to make good use of such help, we need to prepare, prepare, and prepare again. So, there is no rush to find a guru. Most of us need a lot of preparation to undermine our self-centeredness and develop positive psychological qualities.

This universe is marvellously orchestrated. When a guru has become necessary in the course of our spiritual discipline, he or she will be found. We are never alone anyway. Help comes to us all the time from all kinds of sources, including the subtle or higher realms. Some people are desperately seeking their guru, but this is often little more than a self-centered wish. We ought to relax and live life as best we can, practice Yoga as best we can, and patiently wait for the guru to appear.

We have stopped recommending teachers, because it has been our experience that seekers want to seek rather than find. They might not even recognize their guru when they see him or her. In the past, our recommendations were typically ignored. More instructive have been those cases where contact with the guru proved somehow impossible, even though he or she may have lived conveniently close to a seeker. Usually, the seeker gives up trying to connect with the guru after a number of failed attempts, or becomes sidetracked by other attractive opportunities. One must conclude that a meeting was not meant to happen just then.

16. I find "living liberation" difficult to understand. How can I begin to wrap my mind around this idea?

"Living liberation" is for sure a challenging concept. Liberation is something that happens from the viewpoint of the mind. Our innermost essence is always liberated, or free. Think of the mind as a screen in front of a bright light. That screen can be either opaque, hardly allowing any of the light through at all, or it can be completely translucent, so that the light rays are scarcely blocked. In most cases, the screen of the mind is some shade in between these two extremes, depending on one's spiritual development. Through the steadfast practice of Yoga, we can gradually remove the darker screens and thus permit the light of ultimate Awareness into our mind and being. At one point, there occurs a radical switch in us. Instead of identifying with our mind and personality, we wake up as the unchanging essence, or Awareness, which we have always been.

Many Yoga masters maintain that while we are alive in the world, there will always be a screen between us and our true essence. But that screen is completely transparent and completely "seen through," so that it is still possible to speak of Self-realization. When a Self-realized master dies, this final screen simply drops away and full liberation is the case. Essentially, then, liberation is the same before and after death. Some teachers speak of "living liberation" also as enlightenment, while others equate enlightenment with full or post-mortem liberation. It makes no difference really.

17. Some forms of Yoga seem to accept a belief in God, while others don't. How should we understand this?

This is true. Bhakti-Yoga very much assumes the existence of God, who is understood as a superperson. Jnana-Yoga, by contrast, speaks of the ultimate Self, or essence, instead. But it also admits of a creator-deity who emerges ("is born") out of the ultimate, lives for a very long time, and then "dies." When the creator dies, the universe disintegrates. After a period of time (in human terms), the creator-deity emerges again out of the ultimate and then gives rise to a new universe. Thus, the creation and destruction of the universe is regarded as happening in cycles.

The creator is named Brahma, who is often confused with the Absolute and impersonal *brahman*, or ultimate essence of everything. In Christian mystical terms, this contrast is captured in the difference between God and Godhead. The Godhead goes beyond personhood, which is why some (but by no means all) practitioners of Jnana-Yoga address Brahma but not the impersonal *brahman* when they want to pray for help. Whether we think of Brahma as an actual deity or as a psychological device (or archetype), he is clearly a helpful threshold figure.

Yogins are not so arrogant as to dismiss help from deities. They don't have to combat the intellectual bias of atheism, which prevents the mind from experiencing the full spectrum of realities. So, positive thinking, openness, and prayer are very much part of the vocabulary of Yoga.

18. If the *yogis* are so realistic and have such great mastery over their minds, including the unconscious, why do they believe in many deities?

This question implies that the deities acknowledged in Hinduism are fictional or have only a psychological reality. Briefly, this is little more than an intellectual assumption, that is, an opinion. Since the *yogins* are indeed realists and come to know the workings of the mind in fine detail, would it not be more reasonable to assume that they speak from experience? If they claim that there are deities, just as there are many subtle (normally invisible) levels of existence, they are not merely fantasizing. They encounter certain living qualities that their mind steeped in Hindu symbolism experiences in specific ways. The *yogins* know full well that they must go far beyond these deities, or angels. They must go beyond even Brahma in order to realize the essence of everything.

The *yogins* experience the universe quite differently from the ordinary person. Because Westerners basically believe in a "flat-land" universe—consisting only of matter—they have effectively banished all paranormal realities into oblivion. To put it starkly, Westerners would tend to see aliens and flying saucers, while other more traditionally-minded people would see living qualities like deities, or angels. (That is not to deny the idea of other biological life forms in the universe, some of whom may be in contact with Earth.)

19. Is it okay to charge for Yoga instruction? Should Yoga teachers not offer classes for free?

Yoga teachers, like other teachers, are professionals, and by and large they teach to make a living in addition to communicating useful knowledge or skills. To expect that they teach for free is not realistic in our society. Like everyone else, they have to pay for the studio space, take care of their rent or mortgage, make car payments, and put food on the table. Long ago, when Georg was first offering posture classes, he decided one day not to charge, assuming that students would make a donation "from the heart." This was not at all the case, and with having to travel from one end of London to the other, he sometimes was barely able to pay for the rented room. He stopped his unreasonable practice very quickly.

There is nothing wrong with charging for Yoga instruction. We would hope, however, that all Yoga centers have regular free classes for the financially stressed, and for the elderly and debilitated people. They will be grateful beneficiaries.

Understand that the contemporary Yoga movement is still "in the making," and has much to learn. With few exceptions, Yoga teachers need better training. Better training means acquiring a sturdy background in the spiritual teachings of Yoga. This often falls under the category of "philosophy" in Yoga teacher-training programs. Often this amounts to very little. In any case, Yoga philosophy without spirituality is meaningless. Some Yoga instructors confuse New Age thought with Yoga spirituality and we feel this could be remedied by ensuring Yoga teacher training have a stronger Yoga philosophy component. To address this issue, Georg wrote a Yoga philosophy teacher training manual which is being used in several countries around the world and Brenda offers an online Yoga philosophy program for students and teachers who feel they would like to learn a bit more about this important aspect of Yoga. Don't hesitate to quiz a Yoga teacher before signing on. We recommend you asking if they studied Yoga philosophy in their teacher training; if they are continuing their Yoga philosophy studies; and how they apply that wisdom in their classes. Spirituality is the alpha and omega of Yoga!

20. Recently I participated in a Yoga class in southern California. I was shocked to see women dressed in rather skimpy and provocative outfits. No one seemed to mind. Is this normal?

This may be acceptable to some, but it is definitely not acceptable from the perspective of traditional Yoga or even common sense. We guess that Yoga teachers are reluctant to demand respectable clothing in class because this might reduce attendance. Some studios have started to introduce a dress code, and no one seems to object. We think Yoga students, even if they are only interested in postural practice, should be obliged to wear a decent outfit to class, and also show respectful behavior otherwise. Yoga teachers, again, should not be afraid to set certain standards. The ethical guidelines we have drawn up, which are available for free at www.traditionalyogastudies.com, suggest such standards at least for Yoga teacher trainees.

In any case, when we participate in a Yoga class, we should use our attendance as an occasion to altogether transform our mindset, which includes our everyday behavior. Besides, we are not in a Yoga class to catch someone's eyes or to make a fashion statement, but simply to practice.

21. The Yoga studio that I normally go to is forever marketing Yoga products. In class, teachers recommend that everyone checks out the items available in the lobby, and whenever I arrive, the woman in the lobby always points out the latest gadgets. This is quite annoying, and I am loath to go there now even though the practice space is appealing. Any comments?

Western Yoga has become thoroughly commercialized, and Yoga is sold as a commodity along with Yoga-related gadgets. Some centers market aggressively, because there is money to be made. You are quite rightly put off by this. You can either express your feelings to the owner or simply choose to not buy into the commercialization and not purchase products from the studio.

22. I find it disturbing that so many studios play music during class. Who started this trend and how can one stop it?

We have no idea how playing music in a Yoga class became fashionable—and it *is* fashionable. Maybe this habit is a carryover from fitness classes, which is what Yoga is for many people. There is the lockstep kind of music, and then there is the dreamy stuff. It is definitely all distracting and defeats the purpose of traditional Yoga practice. Unfortunately, we don't think you or we can stop it, because too many people actually like being distracted that way. We recommend talking to the instructor or studio owner and asking if there is a class that is more suited to your needs.

23. Where can I find spiritually-based Yoga classes? I am at a loss.

Sadly, such classes are not common, and we can't make any recommendations. Often classes associated with an ashram (a traditional Yoga school) have a spiritual slant. But they may also tend toward the sectarian. Your best bet is to ask around. If you don't see the word "spiritual" or "transformative" in an ad, you may be less likely to find this approach when you go to the center.

24. I used to enjoy Partner Yoga. Then, when I relocated and had to go to a different center which did not offer Partner Yoga, I came to enjoy a more quiet, inward-looking Yoga practice. I am wondering whether I am becoming more self-centered?

Partner Yoga is a modern invention. Having observed classes in Partner Yoga, we know we could never go this way. Just because you prefer a more quiet Yoga practice now doesn't mean you are becoming self involved. Not at all. When you look at Patanjali's definition of posture, you will see that it is meant to be accompanied by relaxation and what he calls "coinciding with the infinite." This last qualification implies that one should practice posture with great mindfulness. Another way of speaking about this is "looking inward" and calmly observing what is going on in the body and mind. This does not seem to be a prominent feature in Partner Yoga.

We, too, enjoy a quiet posture practice. Partner Yoga can be quite distracting. Certainly, your mental focus is not on what is going on in your *own* body and mind. And, if you don't know or don't trust your partner, you may be worrying whether he or she will accidentally let go of you and cause an injury. Or you may worry that you might do the same to your partner when it is your turn to assist. Also mixed-gender Partner Yoga is unappealing for us because it involves close physical proximity, the kind you might normally have with a spouse. This can lead to flirting and more serious, if furtive, sexual fooling around. We cannot recommend Partner Yoga for all these reasons. It is not an aspect of traditional Yoga, which favors individual practice.

The question is always: What are we ourselves trying to accomplish? If we seek to grow spiritually, which is a perfectly legitimate goal, then we should look for classes that meet our inner need for quiet and focusing. Don't settle for less.

25. Where in India should I go to learn Yoga properly?

India, we are told, has become so Westernized that many Yoga classes in the cities are now as good or as bad as in the West. Georg never had to travel to the subcontinent, because his teachers always showed up where he happened to live and remained long enough for him to benefit from their teachings. (The only Indian teacher he ever wanted to meet was the great master Ramana Maharshi. He would have followed him anywhere, but Ramana had died in 1950, many years before Georg got to know about him. We both would also journey far afield for our present teacher. Although we don't see him often, we feel he is always somehow with us, and his benign presence in our life has put the capstone on the whole adventure of Yoga.)

"Proper" Yoga is spiritual Yoga. Teachers and schools exist, but they are, we would say, few and far between even in India, and we would not want to recommend specific ones. If you have the idea of studying Yoga directly from one of the "Himalayan" masters, you might be disappointed. Many genuine guru*s* are loath to take on Western disciples, who tend to be self-centered, anti-authoritarian, and insubordinate. And traditional gurus teach in a traditional way, which may rub a practitioner from our part of the world the wrong way.

If you want to learn posture practice, you might be better off with a Western teacher who knows the ins and outs of our Western lifestyle and therefore also our physical limitations. Again, you need to find out for yourself which "style" suits your needs best.

Most importantly, your guru will definitely find you when the time has come!

26. You and your wife have written two books called *Green Yoga* and *Green Dharma.* Have you any additional comments about Yoga's role in creating a healthier environment?

Green Yoga, which was published in 2007, provided an uncompromising overview of the problems with the ecosystem. We felt that people had been given bits and pieces and didn't have the larger picture. How else could one explain the almost universal indifference? Some readers were very upset with us, because of our head-on approach. Subsequently, we realized that this confrontation was not helpful and edited the book to offer readers a more user-friendly approach. In addition, we wrote, *Green Dharma,* about Buddhist Yoga vis-à-vis the environment, making essentially the same arguments. As of today, Green Dharma has been downloaded over 100,000 times, which is a respectable figure.

Since only a couple of hundred dollars were donated, we have had to begin charging a minute dollar amount for this and other "free" books, which every person with a computer can afford and which will reimburse us for the time invested in producing this book.

There is no question in our mind that Yoga (in whatever form) can play a major role in transforming our mind, including our current lackadaisical attitude toward the present-day environmental emergency. Yoga practitioners have traditionally been benignly disposed toward the environment, and their sparse lifestyle has been demonstrably conservative rather than consumerist. According to Yoga, we are here on Earth to realize our essence, not to ransack the precious resources we have at our disposal to survive at the physical level. We clearly must change our ways and adopt an environment-friendly outlook. At this late hour, we must make our lifestyle sustainable, which we realize is a tall but absolutely necessary order. All of us are actively harming Nature and our fellow beings by living more or less selfishly and consuming as if there is no tomorrow. (Well, at the present rate of consumption, there will be "no tomorrow" for us and most other life forms.)

Our two books—*Green Yoga* and *Green Dharma*—were intended as passionate pleas for everyone to accept responsibility as beings who *share* the same planet with a multitude of other beings. Those beings are our neighbours and have an equal right to live here. If we allow the extinction rate (now reckoned to be roughly 150 plant and animal *species* per day) to continue, our own species will blink out. Earth, biologists warn us, will be plunged back into the Cambrian era of 600-million years ago—an unthinkable prospect.

27. I heard in a seminar that the ego must be killed before enlightenment can happen. Is this true?

Some traditional teachers talk in this way. Our own view, which is also based on tradition, is that enlightenment occurs when the ego is transcended, or gone beyond, rather than killed, or destroyed, outright. Many traditions maintain that enlightenment is possible prior to death. If that's so—and, based on the testimony of numerous adepts—we believe it is, then we must also assume that the ego has to be present. Without an ego to navigate this body-mind, we would be a sorry sight indeed. We think we couldn't live without the ego-pilot. Of course, the ego of the enlightened master is a shadow of its former self. It has not an ounce of egotism left in it. Thoroughly transformed, it is stripped of all the stuff that makes the ordinary person tick. What a paradoxical but marvellous condition this is! We hope we all can reach it one day.

28. Why is it that we hear a lot about ancient male Yoga teachers who have written Sanskrit books but no woman teachers who are also authors?

Female Yoga teachers were by no means rare in earlier times; they just did not write texts like intellectually-minded teachers of the ilk of Patanjali, Vyasa, or Vidyaranya. Not that females were necessarily illiterate. They just did not feel the need to express their thoughts in writing, as did Lalla in the Kashmiri language during the Middle Ages. For the longest time, women were sought after as teachers—or gurus—notably in the Tantric tradition. They knew that spiritual transmission happened rarely through the medium of books. Much better for their disciples, we'd say!

29. How can I make posture practice a *spiritual* affair?

We'd say that it all depends on the context. If the context is spiritual, so will be your posture (*asana*) practice. This includes approaching the postures mindfully (that is, with awareness) and reasonably slowly. Don't just whip out your mat and get going. Center yourself first. Relaxation, at least at the end of a session, is important, too. And don't forget to sit quietly in meditation to conclude your session. Even five minutes of meditation will work miracles over time. It really doesn't matter that the mind is racing to begin with. Focus on the breath going in and out of your nose, or use whatever concentration technique works for you.

30. I have a Buddhist meditation practice and also do Hatha-Yoga postures occasionally. Do they conflict with each other?

Only you are able to answer this question. If you don't feel a conflict mixing traditions, you are fine. Buddhism has its own postural practices. They are more vigorous than the postures of Hindu Yoga, but this is not a problem in itself. Some systems, such as the *Kum Nye* postural system, draws from the training and experience of the Buddhist teacher Tarthang Tulku, and seems to connect students with that lineage in a more subtle way.

Please, don't just *do* the postures, as so many people say, but *practice* or *cultivate* them. In other words, take them seriously—as seriously as your meditation practice. Then they will work for you! We can wholeheartedly recommend the groundbreaking book *Mindfulness Yoga* by Frank Jude Boccio (Wisdom Publications, 2004) for which Georg wrote a foreword. Frank seeks to bridge the apparent gulf between Buddhism and the postures of Hatha-Yoga.

APPENDIXES

Appendix A: Guide to Sanskrit Pronunciation

Sanskrit is a difficult language to learn and one that, at least for most Westerners, is virtually impossible to master. The pronunciation of its rich vocabulary with its strange sounds is just as difficult. Scholars devised a variety of transliteration schemes to indicate the correct sound of each letter of the alphabet. Then, at a conference of Orientalists held in Athens in 1912, the Sanskrit transliteration was standardized and has been in use since.

We have not availed ourselves of the academic or even simplified transliteration of Sanskrit terms in the present book, which is intended for the complete novice. But in Georg's other books, he has used either full academic or simplified transliteration. The latter recognizes merely the long vowel sounds: ā, ī, and ū. You might bear this in mind. So, don't be surprised when you see *yoginī* (rather than simply *yogini*) or *āsana* (rather than simply *asana*) for a physical posture in some books.

All vowels are to be pronounced open, like in Italian or Latin. Thus, *yoga* is pronounced with an *o*, as in *short*. The commonly used word *cakra*, which means "wheel," is pronounced *tshakra* rather than *shakra*. The word *mandala*, or "circle," is pronounced with short *a*-sounds, and the emphasis is on the first syllable, not like *mandahla*, with a long middle *a* that is emphasized.

A common mispronunciation concerns the word *Hatha-Yoga*. The *th*-sound is not at all like the English *th* in *this* or *that*. Rather, all consonants followed by an *h* are to be pronounced distinctly as aspirates, as in *top-heavy*. Consequently, *Hatha* is properly pronounced at *Hat-ha* (whereby the first *a* is similar to the *a*-sound in *hut*, not as in *hand*). The common word *phala*, or "fruit," is pronounced *p-hala*, not *fala*, and *kapha* ("phlegm") is pronounced *kap-ha* and not *kafa*. These explanations should help you avoid the worst blunders.

Appendix B: What to Read and Study Next?

With an assortment of Georg's books on Yoga in print, many students are wondering just how to proceed most sensibly with studying his work. This appendix aims at answering the above question.

If you are unfamiliar with the philosophical and spiritual basis of Yoga, which is our primary concern, and are mainly interested in practicing the physical techniques, we suggest that you begin with *Yoga For Dummies Second Edition,* which is coauthored with California Yoga teacher Larry Payne. First published in 1999, this book has served more than 100,000 readers thus far.

When the original publisher (IDG Books) first invited Georg to write this book, he declined without any hesitation. He had his plate full, and he also felt neither interested nor particularly qualified to produce a popular work that would focus on postures. But, to her credit, the acquisitions editor at the time persisted and approached Georg twice more. He thought that her invitation deserved at least his genuine consideration, and it occurred to him that this book would give him an opportunity to at least briefly present the spiritual aspects of Yoga to a wide readership. So, in the end, he agreed to take on this project. He was able to enlist Larry Payne, who has taught the physical techniques over many years, as his collaborator.

In 2009, Larry and Georg were asked by the new publisher (Wiley) to revise the book. Although they both felt that, apart from some minor corrections, it was not in need of revision, they complied with the request. The second edition, published two years later, is again a reliable and easily understandable guide.

If you have read *Yoga For Dummies* and find yourself drawn to the philosophical-spiritual side of Yoga, we can next recommend that you start your further exploration with *The Teachings of Yoga*—an anthology published by Shambhala in 1997 or with *Gems of Yoga,* which is a similar book published by Bantam House in 2002. Alternatively, you might want to listen to Georg's CD

Yoga Wisdom or the CD set (of six CDs) entitled *The Lost Teachings of Yoga,* both published by Sounds True.

Next, at a slightly more demanding level, there is the book *The Path of Yoga* (formerly *The Shambhala Guide to Yoga*), published in a revised edition in 2011. You might then want to turn to *The Deeper Dimension of Yoga*, also released by Shambhala in 2003. This book contains seventy-eight essays, which are reasonably simple-to-understand. Which written over many years, they address a wide range of topics. Arranged in five parts, the essays gradually take you from simple, orienting materials—such as "What is Yoga?" and "Forty Types of Yoga"—to essays on spiritual practice, to considerations about the moral foundation of Yoga, more demanding treatments of the spectrum of Yoga practice, and, finally, to essays on the higher stages of Yoga, such as meditation, prayer, ecstasy, the enigmatic serpent-power (*kundalinī-shakti*), and spiritual liberation.

Yoga: The Deeper Dimension makes an excellent platform for delving into *The Yoga Tradition,* which is a large-size, illustrated volume of well over 500 pages with a foreword by Professor Subhash Kak. It has been called the "Yoga telephone book" by some students, and we can see why. It covers a huge territory and was designed to be used as a comprehensive (though by no means exhaustive) reference work. First published in 1998, this book grew out of Georg's *Yoga: The Technology of Ecstasy,* which is no longer in print. A revised and expanded edition of *The Yoga Tradition* was published in 2008. This volume consists of eighteen chapters arranged in four parts, and it includes his translation of several major Sanskrit texts on Yoga, notably Patanjali's *Yoga-Sutra,* as well as selections from other texts.

The *Yoga-Sutra* is an important text, and in the West is the most studied of all the Sanskrit works on Yoga. Georg translated this text twice: First in his book *The Yoga-Sūtra of Patañjali,* published in 1979 and reissued in 1989 by Inner Traditions, and second in his recent book *The Yoga-Sūtra: A Nondualist Interpretation.* Both works have been released as e-books in 2011 by Traditional Yoga Studies. The latter publication includes detailed grammatical information for those wishing to study this text in the original.

Those wishing to delve yet deeper into the ocean of Yoga may want to participate in Georg's 800-hour distance-learning course accompanying *The Yoga Tradition.* The course comprises nearly 1000 pages, which together with the book represents a small library of several volumes. Thus far, several hundred students from around the world have braved this course, and many have graduated with a certificate of completion. This course represents the culmination of Georg's publications that aim to give Yoga enthusiasts a thorough overview of the philosophy, history, and literature of Yoga covering a period of 5,000 years. We are constantly trying to make the study of this work more accessible, so that students can benefit from it spiritually.

Our other distance-learning courses, all written by Georg, go into more detail on certain aspects addressed in the 800-hour course. Thus, the 250-hour, 380-page course entitled *The Foundations of Yoga* deals with the materials found in Chapters 1–8 in his book *The Yoga Tradition.* There is also a 250-hour, 380-page course entitled *Classical Yoga,* which expands on Chapters 9 and 10, and is based on his translation of Patanjali`s text. The 125-hour, 305-page course entitled *The Bhagavad-Gītā* expands on his recent translation of, and commentary on, this widely read work, published in 2011 by Shambhala. Finally, a 250-hour course on the philosophy and theory of Hatha-Yoga is in preparation.

At some point along this route of self-study, students of Georg's work might want to acquire a copy of his *Encyclopedia of Yoga and Tantra,* which is the 2011 revised and expanded edition of his *Shambhala Encyclopedia of Yoga.* The new version contains well over 2,000 entries and should meet most readers' lexicographic needs or curiosity.

Among Georg's other significant works relating to Yoga, we can point to *The Philosophy of Classical Yoga,* which is an academic monograph on Patanjali`s system published by Manchester University Press (Great Britain) in 1980 and reissued by Inner Traditions (U.S.A.) without modifications in 1996. Then there is *Holy Madness,* published in a revised and expanded edition by Hohm Press in 2006. This book, which has a foreword by psychiatrist Prof. Roger Walsh, M.D., addresses the important subject of guru*s* and spiritual discipleship.

Next we must mention *Yoga Morality,* which is our favorite book. It confronts the most neglected area of Yoga, which is its ethics, and applies the moral principles to modern life. Finally, there is Georg's book *Tantra: The Art of Ecstasy,* which seeks to clarify this much-misinterpreted and complex tradition.

Of coauthored works, we are glad to mention *Green Yoga* and *Green Dharma* (with Brenda) and *In Search of the Cradle of Civilization* (with Subhash Kak and David Frawley). The former two volumes address pressing environmental issues, while the last-mentioned book looks at the early history of Yoga. We feel fortunate to have been able to produce the coauthored volumes together.

SELECT BIBLIOGRAPHY

For more titles by Georg Feuerstein, see Appendix B of this book.

Andrews, Cecile. *Slow Is Beautiful: New Visions of Community, Leisure and Joie de Vivre.* Gabriola Island, Canada: New Society Publishers, 2006.

Baur, Gene. *Farm Sanctuary: Changing Hearts and Minds about Animals and Food.* New York: Touchstone, 2008.

Benson, Herbert with Miriam Z. Klipper. *The Relaxation Response.* New York: Avon Books, 1975.

Boccio, Frank Jude. *Mindfulness Yoga: The Awakened Union of Breath, Body, and Mind.* Boston, Mass.: Wisdom Publications, 2004.

Cousens, Gabriel. *Conscious Eating.* Berkeley, Calif.: North Atlantic Books, 2000.

Craig, Mary. *Kundun: A Biography of the Family of the Dalai Lama.* Washington, D.C.: Counterpoint, 1997.

Dechanet, J. M. *Christian Yoga.* London: Search Press, 1973.

De Michelis, Elizabeth. *A History of Modern Yoga.* London: Continuum, 2004.

Dobson, Charles. *The Troublemaker's Teaparty: A Manual for Effective Citizen Action.* Gabriola Island. B.C.: New Society Publishers, 2001.

Feuerstein, Brenda. *The Yoga-Sūtra from a Woman's Perspective.* Eastend, Canada: Traditional Yoga Studies, 2011. (E-book)

__________, Brenda. *Yoga Sleep (Yoga-Nidrā).* Eastend, Canada: Traditional Yoga Studies, 2011. (CD)

Feuerstein, Georg. *The Lost Teachings of Yoga.* Boulder, Colo.: Sounds True, 2002. (set of 6 CDs)

__________ and Brenda Feuerstein. *Green Dharma.* Eastend, Canada: Traditional Yoga Studies, 2009.

__________ and Brenda Feuerstein. *Green Yoga.* Eastend, Canada: Traditional Yoga Studies, 2007.

Goodall, Jane. *Harvest of Hope: A Guide to Mindful Eating.* New York: Wellness Central/Hatchette, 2006.

Iyengar, B. K. S. *The Tree of Yoga.* Boston, Mass.: Shambhala Publications, 1989.

Lasater, Judith. *Living Your Yoga: Finding the Spiritual in Everyday Life.* Berkeley, Calif.: Rodmell Press, 2000.

Lommel, Pim van. *Consciousness Beyond Life: The Science of the Near-Death Experience.* New York: HarperCollins, 2010.

Merkel, Jim. *Radical Simplicity: Small Footprints on a Finite Earth.* Gabriola Island, Canada: New Society Publishers, 2003.

Murphy, Michael. *The Future of the Body: Exploration into the Further Evolution of Human Nature.* Los Angeles: J. P. Tarcher, 1992.

Nagapriya. *Exploring Karma & Rebirth.* Birmingham, England: Windhorse Publications, 2004.

Robbins, John. *A Diet for New America.* Tiberon, Calif.: H. J. Kramer, repr. 1998.

Schweitzer, Albert. *The Teaching for Reverence for Life.* New York: Holt, Rinehart and Winston, 1965.

Sivananda, Swami. *All About Hinduism.* Shivanandanagar, India: Divine Life Society, 1965.

Suzuki, David and Holly Dressel. *Good News for a Change: How Everyday People are Helping the Planet.* Vancouver, British Columbia: Greystone Books, 2003.

Tart, Charles T. *Waking Up: Overcoming the Obstacles to Human Potential.* Boston, Mass.: Shambhala Publications, 1986.

Terhune, Lea. *Karmapa: The Politics of Reincarnation.* Boston, Mass.: Wisdom Publications, 2004.

Walsh, Roger. *Staying Alive: The Psychology of Human Survival.* Boulder, Co. and London: New Science Library/ Shambhala, 1984.

_________ and Frances Vaughan, eds. *Paths Beyond Ego.* Los Angeles: Jeremy Tarcher/Perigee, 1993.

Weber, Karl, ed. *Food, Inc.:* New York: PublicAffairs, 2009.

White, John, ed. *What Is Meditation?* Garden City, N.Y.: Doubleday/Anchor Original, 1974.

ESSENTIAL SANSKRIT GLOSSARY

Most Hindu Yoga texts are written in Sanskrit, but also in Tamil and various vernacular Indian languages, such as Bengali and Gujarati. To follow conversations at Yoga studios, you need to know some Sanskrit words. The following list probably includes more words than you will hear. For a full dictionary, please consult Georg's *Encyclopedia of Yoga and Tantra* (revised and enl. ed. 2011).

Abhyasa – lit. "repetition," practice

Acarya – preceptor

Adhyatma-Yoga – Yoga of the inner self

Advaita Vedanta – the philosophical system of radical non-dualism, usually associated with the name of the great teacher **Shankara.**

Aghori – member of an extremist Tantric sect, which was made famous by author and practitioner Robert Svoboda in his trilogy.

Aham brahmasmi – "I am the Absolute" (*aham* + *brahma* + *asmi*); a classic saying of Vedanta

Ahamkara – lit. "I-maker"; the ego

Ahimsa – non-violence, or non-harming; a cardinal virtue of Yoga practitioners; one of the first **yamas**

Akasha – space, or ether; as in "akashic record"

Amrita – nectar, also immortality

Anahata-cakra – the **cakra** of the "unstruck" (*anahata*) sound at the heart

Ananda – bliss

Anga – lit. "limb"; a category of the yogic path; thus, **Patanjali** distinguishes eight members

Anjali-mudra – the gesture of placing the palms of the hands together in front of the heart in order to salute or simply greet someone

Asamprajnata-samadhi – lit. "supraconscious ecstasy"; the highest form of ecstasy in the eightfold path of **Patanjali;** the equivalent of **nirvikalpa-samadhi**

Asana – lit. "seat"; a yogic posture, or pose; There are too many *asanas* to list them here individually.

Ashrama – often pronounced **ashram**; a hermitage or, nowadays, a school of Yoga

Ashtanga-Yoga – a modern style of Hatha-Yoga; another name of **Patanjali**'s Classical Yoga of eight limbs

Atman – the transcendental Self

AUM – another way of writing *om.*

Bandha – lit. "bondage," or "lock"; in the latter sense, the word refers to a threefold technique by which the breath is stopped within the body

Bhagavad-Gita – lit. "Lord's Song"; this is a widely read Yoga text

Bhakti – lit. "devotion," especially between Krishna and his devotees; hence Bhakti-Yoga

Bhastrika – one of the breathing techniques of Hatha-Yoga

Bija (bija) – lit. "seed"; sometimes precedes the word **mantra**

Brahmacarya – lit. "brahmic conduct"; the discipline of chastity

Brahman – the Absolute, often understood as the Divine in impersonal form; the transcendental core of the world, which is identical with the **atman**

Brahmana – a Hindu belonging to the priestly class

Buddhi – the higher, intuitive mind, as opposed to reason

Cakra – lit "wheel"; often spelled *chakra* and mispronounced *shakra;* Hindu Yoga knows of a series of seven cakras; Buddhist Yoga knows five

Candra – the moon; also the internal structure that oozes the nectar of immortality

Citta – the mind

Dana – generosity, gift; usually, an offering to the teacher in addition to whatever fee is charged

Deva – God, godling; in the latter sense, a *deva* has the function of an angel

Devi – the Mother Goddess, such as **Kali**

Dharma – virtue, righteousness; quality, also teaching

Dhyana – meditation; often mispronounced *diana*

Drishti – "view" or "gaze"; a way of gazing during meditation

Gayatri – a famous **mantra** of Hinduism

Gheranda-Samhita – lit. "Gheranda's Collection;" one of three major texts of traditional Hatha-Yoga

Goraksha – lit. "cow protector," but this name is likely to mean "someone who keeps his tongue"; the founder of Hatha-Yoga

Guna – lit. "strand" or "quality"; in Hindu Yoga and Samkhya, one of three fundamental constituents of the cosmos: *sattva, rajas,* and *tamas*

Guru – lit. "heavy" or "weighty"; a spiritual teacher

Hatha – lit. force; this word is frequently mispronounced with the English *th* instead of the Sanskrit aspirated sound *t-h;* esoterically, it signifies but does not literally mean "sun and moon" whereby *ha* stands for the sun and *tha* for the moon

Hatha-Yoga – the Yoga of physical transformation consisting esoterically in the union of sun and moon

Hatha-Yoga-Pradipika – lit. "Light on the Forceful Yoga"; one of three classic Sanskrit texts on Hatha-Yoga

Ida or **ida-nadi** – lit. "channel of comfort"; the conduit of the life force that proceeds through the left nasal passage; cf. **pingala**

Ishvara – lit. "the lord"; God

Jalandhara – one of the three **bandha**s

Japa – recitation of a **mantra,** often with a rosary

Jiva – psyche, or soul

Jnana – knowledge, wisdom

Kali – lit. "she who impels"; a form of the Goddess

Kali-yuga – the present dark era; the word *kali* is not related to the name of the Goddess

Karma – lit. "action"; the stem of the word is *karman;* it can stand for either "activity" or "destiny"

Kula – lit. "family"

Kirtana – lit. "chanting"; the common practice of singing songs of praise

Klesha – lit. "trouble"; according to **Patanjali,** the *kleshas* are the root of the karmic legacy deep within the mind

Krishna – lit. "puller"; one of the incarnations of the Divine in Vaishnavism

Kriya – lit. "action" or "ritual"; also an involuntary body movement in **Kundalini-Yoga**

Kumbhaka – lit. "potlike"; retention of the breath

Kundalini or **kundalini-shakti** – lit. "coiled power"; the psychospiritual energy residing in potential form in the lowest **cakra**

Kundalini-Yoga – the practice of awakening the **kundalini** and guiding it to the topmost **cakra** at the crown of the head

Lakshmi – a name of the Goddess

Linga – lit. "mark" or "sign"; phallus; the creative sign of **Shiva**

Maithuna – lit. "twinning"; sacred sexual intercourse in Tantra

Manas – the lower mind, reasoning

Mandala – lit. "circle"; a geometric design for focusing the mind

Mantra – a potent sound

Maya – lit. “she who measures”; illusion

Moksha – lit. “liberation”; spiritual freedom, or enlightenment

Mudra – lit. “seal”; a hand gesture or bodily pose similar to **asana**

Mukti – lit. “release”; the same as **moksha**

Nada – the subtle inner sound

Nadi – lit. “conduit”; a subtle channel through or along which the life force (**prana**) travels

Nauli – lit. “rolling”; a technique of **Hatha-Yoga** by which the abdominal muscles are rotated for intestinal cleansing

Neti – one of the cleansing techniques of **Hatha-Yoga** in which water is sucked up the nose, or which uses a thin thread for this purpose

Nidra – sleep; cf. **yoga-nidra**

Nirodha – the control of the mind

Nirvana – lit. “windstill”; the state of enlightenment in which all desires are gone beyond

Nirvikalpa-samadhi – the higher form of ecstasy in which there is no mental activity; cf. **samadhi**

Paramahansa or -**hamsa** – lit. “supreme swan”; the highest type of an ascetic, who has utterly renounced the world

Patanjali – the presumed author of the ***Yoga-Sutra***

Pingala or **pingala-nadi** – the conduit of the life force that proceeds through the right nasal passage; cf. **ida**

Prakriti – lit. “creatrix”; in Classical Yoga and Samkhya, the entire cosmos, as opposed to Spirit (i.e., **purusha**)

Prana – the life force inside and outside the body

Pranayama – lit. "lengthening of the breath"; yogic breath control

Purusha – lit. "man"; in Classical Yoga and Samkhya, the Spirit or transcendental Self

Raja-Yoga – lit. "royal Yoga"; the eightfold path of **Patanjali**

Rishi – lit. "seer"; the title of an advanced **yogin**

Sad-Guru – a true teacher, who has attained enlightenment

Samadhi – ecstasy; the last limb of the eightfold path of **Patanjali;** cf. **asamprajnata-samadhi**

Samatva or **samata** – lit. "sameness"; equanimity

Samkalpa – lit. "intention"; the intention set at the beginning of **yoga-nidra**

Samkhya – a cousin of the Yoga tradition

Samsara – lit. "flow"; cyclic existence, the ordinary world

Samskara – lit. "activator"; an unconscious karmic imprint, which resides in the depths of the mind

Samyama – lit. "constraint"; the practice of concentration, meditation, and ecstasy in regard to the same mental object

Satya – lit. "truthfulness"; one of the moral disciplines of Yoga

Samprajnata-samadhi – lit. "conscious ecstasy"; the lower form of ecstasy; cf. **nirvikalpa-samadhi**

Seva – lit. "service"; unselfish service for the teacher or hermitage

Shakti – lit. "power"; generally, the **kundalini**

Shankara – a celebrated teacher of **Advaita Vedanta;** often called Shankaracarya (from Shankara + acarya)

Shanti – lit. "peace"

Shankara – the main preceptor of nondualism (Advaita Vedanta)

Shiva – a name of God

Shiva-Samhita – one of the three classic texts of **Hatha-Yoga**

Siddha – lit. "accomplished one"; an adept

Siddhi – lit. "power" or "accomplishment"; a paranormal ability

Surya – the sun

Surya-Namaskara – lit. "saluting the sun"; an exercise series apparently invented in modern times

Sutra – lit. "aphorism"; a concise statement, as in the ***Yoga-Sutra***

Svamin – lit. "ruler" or "lord"; the spiritual title *swami*

Tantra – lit. "loom"; a particular spiritual tradition or the main texts used by it

Trataka – a technique in **Hatha-Yoga** by which one relaxedly gazes at a flame of light

Upanishads – lit. "sitting near"; category of works teaching **Vedanta**

Vedanta – lit. "Veda's end; the teaching of the *Upanishads*

Viveka – lit. "discernment"; a central practice of Yoga, which seeks to distinguish between the real (i.e. the Self) and the unreal (i.e. the cosmos)

Vritti – lit. "whirl"; one of the main activities of the mind, according to **Patanjali**

Yama – moral discipline, according to **Patanjali**

Yantra – lit. "device"; a geometric design similar to the **mandala,** which is used for concentration

Yoga-nidra – lit. "Yoga sleep," a deep relaxation technique involving auto-suggestion

There are too many *asanas* to list them here individually.

INDEX

A

Absolute, 77. *See also brahman*
adepts, 9, 84
ahimsa, 19
alchemy: Yoga as, 25
Amrita-Bindu-Upanishad, 35
asana,18, 21, 85, 89. *See also* postures
asceticism, 21
atheism, 75
atman, 28
attention, 22, 34, 48, 61
aum. See om
awakening: of *kundalini* 26, 42

B

Bhagavad-Gita, 7, 30, 32, 41, 54, 56, 72, 92, 115
Bhagavata-Purana, 32
bhakti, 32
Bhakti-Sutras, 32
Bhakti-Yoga, 4-5, 32, 33, 67, 77
Boccio, Frank Jude, 85
body: discipline, 21, 43; and upon enlightenment, 43, 44; and food, 61; and Hatha-Yoga, 24, 25; improvement, xiii, 3, 8; and in Karma-Yoga, 30; and liberation, 63; and mindfulness, 81; and in religio-spiritual traditions, 25; and Self, 53; and suffering, 15, 16
bondage, 9, 35, 43

Brahma, 28, 77-78
brahman, 28, 77
branches: of Yoga, 4-5, 14
breath, breathing, 21, 26, 34, 46, 85
breath control: *See pranayama*
Buddhism, 4, 21, 31, 69, 85

C

cakras, 25, 89
chastity, 19-20
Christianity, 25, 32, 67-69
Classical-Yoga, 92. *See also* Raja-Yoga
concentration, 22, 25, 28, 34, 85; *See also dharana*
consciousness, 25, 27, 32, 35, 36, 40, 56
contentment, 10, 21
Cousens, Dr. Gabriel, 61

D

death, 15, 30, 41, 63, 77, 84
deity, 32-33, 77-78
de Michelis, Elizabeth, xiii
depression, 46-47
desire, 11, 44, 48, 49, 52
devotion, 21, 32-33, 67
dharana, 18, 22
dhyana, 18, 22; *See also* meditation.
diet, 24, 46, 61-62, 67, 71
discernment, 13, 28, 31, 47, 64
disciple, 39-42, 44, 49-52, 64, 74-75, 82, 92
discipline: moral, 18-20. *See also yama*
Divine, 32
doubt, 15, 45
dualism, 36

E

eating, 30, 61, 71. *See also* diet.
ecstasy, 22-23, 25, 34, 56, 64, 72, 91. *See also samadhi.*

ego, 30, 43-46, 53-54,74-75, 84
enlightenment, 22-23, 25, 28, 38, 41-46, 52-57, 63, 74, 77, 84. *See also* liberation; Self-realization
equanimity, 16, 50

F

faith, 5, 28, 45, 67-68
fear, 10,15
food, 19. 61-62. *See also* diet; eating

G

Gandhi, Mahatma, 7
Ganesha, 33
God, 19, 21, 32, 36, 63, 75, 77
Goddess, 32
greed, 10, 19-20, 36, 57
guru, 38-42, 45, 49-52, 64, 69, 73-76, 82, 92

H

happiness, 13, 22
harmony, 56
hatha: hidden meaning of, 26
Hatha-Yoga, 4, 24-25, 37, 67, 85, 89, 92
heart, 4, 32-33, 78
Hinduism, 5, 17, 37, 68, 78
history: of Yoga, 92
Hittleman, Richard, xiii
hypnosis, 72-73

I

ignorance, 9, 36, 38
initiation, 74

J

japa, 32
Jnana-Yoga, 4, 5, 27-29, 41, 54, 68, 77

K
kali-yuga, 37
karma, 30, 42, 45
Karma-Yoga, 4-5, 30-32, 37, 67
knowledge: path of, 4, 27-29; *and wisdom*, 56
Krishna, 7, 32, 72
Kum Nye, 85
kundalini, 25-26
kundalini-shakti, 91

L
Lalla, 84
liberation, 17, 22, 27, 28, 35- 38, 43-44, 52, 56-58, 63, 76-77, 91
lineage, 4, 33, 38, 85
loka-samgraha, 7

M
mandala, 89
mantra, 5, 10, 23, 28, 34-37, 64
Mantra-Yoga, 4, 34-35
meditation, 5, 10, 13, 18, 21-22, 25, 34-35, 49, 54, 68, 72, 85, 91
mind: transformation 8-9, 12-13; and mantra, 28, 34-35; and self-discipline, 48-50; and wisdom, 56-58
mindfulness, 37, 73, 81, 85
mystic, 25

N
niyama, 18, 21
nonharming, 19, 24, 62, 70
nonstealing, 19

O
obstacles, 45, 64, 73
om, 34, 43
One; the, 27

P

pain, 15-18, 43
Patanjali, 18-23, 59, 81, 84. *See also Yoga-Sutra*
Payne, Larry, 90
perception, 8
pleasure, 10,46
postures, xiii, xiv, 3, 18, 23-24, 39, 67-70, 85, 90
pranayama, 18, 21
prayer, 77, 91
purification, 12, 21, 24
purity, 21

R

Raja-Yoga, 4-5, 18-24
Rama, 32
Ramana Maharshi, 41, 82
Ramalinga, Swami, 25
reality, 5, 8,9 , 27, 32, 34, 36, 41, 43, 78
recitation, 5, 32, 34, 37
relaxation, xiii, 67, 69, 72, 81, 85
religion, 3, 4, 18, 67-68, 75
renunciation, 28
ritual, 4, 5, 34, 36
Robbins, John, 61

S

samadhi, 18, 22
sangha, 51-52
seals, 24
Self, 27, 28, 36, 45-47, 52-54, 57-58, 63, 64
Self-realization, 42, 44, 46, 47, 53-54, 57-58, 63, 75, 77. *See also* enlightenment; liberation
self-restraint, 21
self-transcendence, 53-54
sense withdrawal, 22
sexuality, 37
Shaivism, 68

Shiva, 32, 34, 68
shraddha, 45
sound, 34-35
spirituality: defined, 3; and Yoga, 5, 12, 60, 68, 71, 79
suffering, 10, 14-17, 31, 45-46, 54
study, 68, 71, 82, 90-92

T
tamas, 102
Tantra-Yoga, 4-5, 36-37, 68
Tarthang Tulku, 85
teachers, 38-39, 52, 59, 74, 78-80, 84. *See also guru*
theft, 20
transference, 42
Transmission: spiritual, 32, 84
truthfulness, 19-20, 59

U
unconscious, 34, 57, 78

V
Vaishnavism, 68
Vedanta, 27-28, 69
Vedanta-Sara, 28
vegetarianism, 24, 61, 71
Vidyaranya, 84
Vishnu, 32, 68
visualization, 5, 25
Vivekananda, Swami, xiii
Vyasa, 84

W
Walsh, M.D., Roger, 92
Weber, Karl, 61
Weintraub, Amy, 46
wisdom, xiv, 9, 27-29, 42, 45, 56-58

Y

yama, 18-20
Yoga: as alchemy, 27; and defined, xiii-xiv, 3-6; and Buddhism, 4, 5; eightfold,18-21, 24; and Hinduism, 4, 37, 68; and Jainism, 4; and modern, xiv, 6, 18, 59-60; and religion, 3-4, 18, 67; and Shaivism, 68; and spirituality, 5, 12, 60, 71, 79; and Vaishnavism, 68
Yoga-Sutra, 5, 7, 18-20, 91
yogin, definition, xiv
yogini, definition, xiv

ABOUT THE AUTHORS

Georg Feuerstein, Ph.D. is a leading voice in the dialogue between East and West and has authored over fifty books, many on Yoga. Among his more important works are *The Yoga Tradition, Encyclopedia of Yoga and Tantra, Tantra: The Path of Ecstasy, The Deeper Dimension of Yoga, The Yoga-Sūtra: A New Translation*, and *Yoga For Dummies* (with Larry Payne).

Georg lived a profoundly productive life of humble service and made a peaceful, conscious exit from this world on Saturday, August 25, 2012 near his home in Southern Saskatchewan. His final transition occurred after a nine-day journey of loving resolution in which he was surrounded and supported by his wife Brenda and many spiritual friends.

His legacy of scholarly contribution to the global Yoga community is vast and awe inspiring, to which we all owe a huge debt of gratitude. His work will be lovingly continued and directed by his spiritual partner, lover, friend and wife, Brenda Feuerstein.

If you wish to express your gratitude with a financial contribution, a scholarship fund to support incarcerated practitioners is being created in Georg's honor. **Please visit our website for more details: www.traditionalyogastudies.com**

Brenda Feuerstein has taught Yoga from a spiritual perspective for many years. She is a former music teacher, and health and fitness consultant. She is the author of *The Yoga-Sūtra from a Woman's Perspective* and has coauthored with her husband Georg: *Green Yoga, Green Dharma, The Bhagavad-Gītā: A New Translation.* She is the Director of Traditional Yoga Studies and maintains the position of distance learning course tutor, mentor and teaches workshops, trainings and lectures worldwide.

ABOUT HOHM PRESS

Hohm Press is committed to publishing books that provide readers with alternatives to the materialistic values of the current culture, and promote self-awareness, the recognition of interdependence, and compassion. Our subject areas include parenting, transpersonal psychology, religious studies, women's studies, the arts and poetry.

Contact Information: Hohm Press, PO Box 4410, Chino Valley, Arizona, 86323; USA; 800-381-2700, or 928-636-3331; email: hppublisher@cableone.net

Visit our website at www.hohmpress.com